D

ENTERED MAR 2 8 2007

STORE WINDOWS
No. 12

STORE WINDOWS
No. 12

Martin M. Pegler

Visual Reference Publications, Inc., New York, NY

Copyright © 2002 by Visual Reference Publications, Inc.

All rights reserved. No part of this book may be reproduced in any form or by any electronic or mechanical means, including information storage and retrieval systems, without permission in writing from the publisher.

Visual Reference Publications, Inc.
302 Fifth Avenue
New York, NY 10001

Distributors to the trade in the United States and Canada
Watson-Guptill
770 Broadway
New York, NY 10003

Distributors outside the United States and Canada
HarperCollins International
10 E. 53rd Street
New York, NY 10022

Library of Congress Cataloging in Publication Data:
Store Windows No. 12

Printed in China
ISBN 1-58471-067-5

Book Design: Judy Shepard

CONTENTS

Introduction 7

Asian Influences 10
Auto Parts 14
Back to School 16
Barnyard Fowl 18
Bees & Butterflies 20
Black & White 22
Boxes & Drawers 26
Branding Burberry 28
Cellophane 30
Child's Play 32
Color 34
Color + Form 38
Corrugated Board 40
Denim/Jeans 42
Doggie in the Window 44
Dog-Gone! 46
Egg-o-Mania 48
Everyday Objects 50
Fall 56
Flower Show 62
Flower Power 64
Floral Arrangements 68
Foil-ed Again 70
Fruits & Veggies 72
Gardens & Gardening 74
Gray 76
Halloween 78
In Print 80
Lights 'n' Lamps 82
Lumber 88
Man's World 90
Mirror Images 96
Mother's Day 98
Music 102
Neon 104

On Stage 106
Overscaled 108
Photography 112
Picture This! 118
Pin-Ups 122
Pink 126
Resort 128
Sale 130
Say it Again 134
Say it Again & Again 136
Say it Again & Again & Again 138
Sew & So 140
Sew What? 142
Sheer Madness 144
Sporting Life 146
Summertime 150
Surreal 154
Swimwear 156
Theater 158
Time & Timepieces 162
Traveling On 164
Urban Look 166
Web-Work 168
Wire Works 170
Wood 172
Wood Works 174

Index 175

INTRODUCTION

It is rare today that one sees a shopper rushing down a shopping street suddenly stop—turn around, and step back to look at a window display. Why? Because window displays that really stop a shopper in his or her tracks just don't happen very often. Where windows once exuded the store's fashion image and the retailer's own brand of panache, today we seem to live in a world where there are too few retail organizations with original presentation concepts and the others are merely clones. Even as scientists found what they could do in a test tube to create exact reproductions, it appears that retailers discovered the technique—in their windows. All they had to do is see what some successful retailer was doing and do the very same—with few variations or changes. Walking through a mall or down a main or market street is often a journey through sameness; a boring, unexciting, repetitious show of drapers, costumers or headless forms backed up by a monster photograph. Where's the fun and the excitement of yesteryear? Where is all the creative talent that is out there? It seems to be wasting from lack of use!

And yet, through every mist there is a ray of light and hope and even thundershowers end up with rainbows. Thus, with diligence, with endless searching and with endless ventures into the retail jungle we have succeeded in coming up with yet another volume of great, attractive and attracting windows that say, "Yes Virginia—there really is Display." The promotions that we have collected are proof that there are still retailers out there who know and understand the value of display. They know how to target their customers with presentations that enhance the product offering while adding luster to their retail business. That is what Display is all about!

Display is an Art—but not an Art for Art's sake. It is an Art form that comfortably and without excuses or apologies serves the retail industry. The "tools" of the artist/designer may vary and as the reader turns the pages of this volume he or she will see realistic mannequins, stylized mannequins and abstract mannequins—mannequins without heads and forms and torsos that are part anatomy and part sculpture. These artists/designers use color; the color of the merchandise and the colors of the lights that enhance, vitalize and add excitement to what may otherwise be a very "Still Life." Color and light add life to the display composition. Costly and one-of-a-kind props or decoratives are rarer than ever because the budgets the artists/designers are given are being forever cut. Imagination and resourcefulness has to take over. Turn these pages and see how the most mundane, ordinary and even trite objects are turned into unique treats for the viewer's eye. See what talented people can do with bits and scraps; pieces of unused lumber—a neglected chair—bottles, boxes and barrels—a broom and a mop. Things that the ordinary person would never see as more than what they actually are, through the magic of Display, are turned into wondrous objects to behold and savor.

I am the eternal optimist. I look for the rosy lining in each gray cloud just as I expect to find something fabulous in every mall I walk through and on each shopping street I travel down. For those of you who turn these pages and I hope will refer back to them over and over again—do not despair. Display is here to stay! It has been around since the earliest artisans and traders set out their wares on colorful carpets under flapping tents in the desert. Even then they knew how to catch the sunlight and let it reflect off their wares. There will always be enlightened retailers who know that to stand out from the sameness surrounding them. They must be different—special—unique. Display will help make them so. Therefore, this volume is dedicated to the enlightened retailers who give the artists/designers the space and the wherewithal to do what they do and to the legions of talented display designers and artists—the established and the well known as well as the many trying to make a name. Some of those "names" are presented in this volume along with the retailers who had the foresight to select them. They are who really make retailing a form of Entertainment.

Martin M. Pegler

STORE WINDOWS
No. 12

HENRI BENDEL, Fifth Ave., New York, NY
Dir. Of Visual Presentation: Graham Belman

"Far away places with strange sounding names"—bazaars—casbahs—spices and scents—rich, searing colors—burnished copper, brass and bronze—delicate calligraphy all spirals, swirls and sweeping brushstrokes—exotic—unique—unusual: these are all Asian Influences and these Asian influences are seen and understood everywhere.

Bendel goes to the bazaars and to the exotic with these windows. The open back, two story high window is filled with richly colored and patterned rugs hanging, draped, folded and spread out. Pierced and patterned copper, brass, and bronze light fixtures are suspended throughout the space to add to the bazaar-like atmosphere. In a smaller window, the carpets are spread out on the floor while the hanging lamps and lanterns carry through the established theme. A Balinese theme is affected in another Bendel display with shadowy artwork on a fan-like background accented by the warm, rich amber, gold and pink lighting on it. The three stylized figures are dressed in brilliantly colored, jewel trimmed garments.

ASIAN INFLUENCES 11

HENRI BENDEL, (RIGHT AND BELOW)
Fifth Ave., New York, NY
Dir. of Visual Presentation: Graham Belman

SHANGHAI TANG: Fifth Ave., New York, NY

HOYA CRYSTAL, Madison Ave, New York, NY
Design: Julin & Larrabee

Shanghai Tang really knows how to speak the Asian Design tongue! In this partially open-back window, the heavily carved wooden wall panels are pulled back to reveal the selling floor in which the theme is carried through with red lanterns, hot pink curved archways and rich, gold-leaf trim. Throughout, hot pink and bright red garments interact— clash and excite—while black is used to unify and gold to highlight. Simple Chinese furniture and colorful silk lanterns add to the truly breath-taking setting.

At Hoya Crystal, the elegant crystal vases are complemented by what looks like Haiku poetry panels that are delicately calligraphed to look like Japanese brush-stroke characters. The stones and gravel and the black lacquered plinths also add a refined Japanese influence.

ASIAN INFLUENCES

SHERLE WAGNER, E. 57th St., New York, NY
Designer: Anne Kong

J. MENDEL, Madison Ave., New York, NY

BERGDORF GOODMAN, Fifth Ave, New York, NY
VP of Visual Presentation: Linda Fargo
Window Director: David Hoey

Bergdorf Goodman creates a fantasy background out of swirling peacock feathers that enhance the presentation of the silk, gold trimmed, saris and the velvet stoles. It is like stepping out of an Arabian Night's Dream.

Sherle Wagner goes Asian with these elegant bathroom fixtures. The red/maroon and gold drapery—rich in calligraphy—appears even more impressive when complemented by the other red fabrics and contrasted with the white. The gold accents and the dramatic lighting also enrich the product presentation.

The fur-trimmed coat in the J.Mendel's window gains in delicacy and in stature from the background panel that seems to have been inspired by a Japanese ink painting on rice paper.

14   STORE WINDOWS   No. 12

BARNEYS, (TOP AND ABOVE) Madison Ave., New York, NY
Creative Director: Simon Doonan
Sr. VP of Creative Services: David New
VP of Creative Services: Adamo DiGregorio

Autos are an integral part of our lives and for some the auto is more than just a means of transportation; it represents a lifestyle. Your "wheels" are who you are and what you hope to be.

Barneys—always in touch with lifestyles and lifestyle visualization—turned their Madison Ave. windows into veritable "chop shops" as they filled them with bits and pieces of autos and auto parts. Added to the actual elements are advertisements, posters and banners of retro autos. All this to celebrate the "Cerruti 1881" collection of menswear.

Bergdorf Men's store created a polka dotted pattern—in depth—with inflated auto tubes. The donuts are lined up and hung in front of the wall which is already patterned with a layer of inner tubes.

Gucci takes a more elegant approach with luxury auto steering wheels used to create an overall pattern on the rich, dark brown wall. Some of Gucci's fashion accessories are perched or set down on the wheels so that fashion can take off in the fast lane.

GUCCI, Fifth Ave., New York, NY
Corp. Dir. of Visual Presentation: James Knight

BERGDORF MEN'S STORE, Fifth Ave., New York, NY
VP of Visual Presentations: Linda Fargo
Visual Presentation Director: David Hoey

It would not be fall if it didn't start with Back to School/College promotions. Of course, it could be time to pull out of storage the red plastic apples, the giant pens and pencils and the oversized, cut-out A-B-Cs—or one could try some more interesting approaches.

Back To School at Marshall Field, in Chicago, was "Destination: Education." To help you get there, in the children's wear windows there were overscaled black and yellow, familiar "School Crossing" signs. These were enhanced by the yellow and black striped horizontal bands also seen at streetside locations. A nice touch is the yellow and black striped rugby shirt on the form in the center. For the High School or College bound crowd, a cluster of yellow painted lockers serves as the background for the semi-abstract figures and a giant, lifestyle photo accents the featured garments.

Bergdorf takes the book—a standard back to school cliché—and turns it into something new and unique. The library vignette would make a memorable setting for any educational or cultural promotion.

Bloomingdale's has found a formula that works for showing off college-bound clothes. The "slate board" or "blackboard" background is covered with chalked on formulas that don't have to make sense—they just look authentic. The two lifestyle mannequins stand stiff and square in front of the "theory" on what the well dressed student will wear.

MARSHALL FIELD
(ABOVE AND RIGHT)
State St., Chicago, IL
V.M. Director, Dayton-Hudson: Jamie Becker
V.M. Manager, State St.: Amy Meadows
Photographer: Susan Kezon:

BACK TO SCHOOL 17

BERGDORF GOODMAN, Fifth Ave., New York, NY
Linda Fargo: VP of Visual Merchandising
David Hoey: Window Director

BLOOMINGDALES, Lexington Ave., New York, NY
VP of Visual Merchandising: Jack Hruska
Creative Director: Mike Fisher
Window Manager: Harry Medina

18 STORE WINDOWS No. 12

DAFFYS, Fifth Ave., New York, NY
Display Director: Mary Costantini

What says summer or casual like a day in the country? What says Country better than a farm, a barn, and a barnyard filled with chicks, geese and sheep? Daffy's gets them all into the window. The background panel has a stylized and decorative rendering of a barnyard setting and the green turf matting covers the floor. All the barnyard denizens fill the floor and surround the two city girls dressed in their going-to-the-country best. Bushels of hay add to the propping of the scene.

To show off some really elegant bath and bedroom furnishings, Sherle Wagner has turned the windows over to the roosters and blue ones at that. They coordinate with the blue prints on the bedroom fabrics and on the artwork on the bathroom porcelain sink and accessories. The totally sophisticated look is further enhanced by the gold colored straw strewn out on the floor. Note the salute to Country with the "good morning" headboard and the use of directional letters off a weather vane atop the forms. "S" and "W" also just happen to stand for Sherle Wagner.

SHERLE WAGNER, (ABOVE AND LEFT) E. 57th St., New York, NY
Designer: **Anne Kong**

MACY'S, Herald Square, New York, NY
Window Visual Director: Sam C. Joseph

Bees are swarming to Macy's Flower Show to meet, greet and "eat" the thousands of nectar-rich flowers on display. Meanwhile the honey-gathering outfits of padded mitts and plastic masks and netting all add interest to the presentation of casual khaki and beige colored men's separates. It's a stinger!

Butterflies come in all colors and shapes and we usually think of them hovering over plants and flowers. At Uhren Huber, in Munich, the black bamboo framed butterflies are backed up with red tissue and set against shocking pink panels. The hot pink is used to cover the pedestal displayers for the jewelry. Together—the red, pink and black turn this into an Asian fantasy.

UHREN HUBER, Munich, Germany
Design & Execution: Peter Rank, DeKo Rank

BEES & BUTTERFLIES 21

At Cecile, in Hamilton, Bermuda, the realistic mannequins are turned into fashion butterflies by the addition of the cut-out cardboard wings inset with "stained glass" pieces of colored tissue. Additional cut out butterfly shapes appear on the walls and on the accessory arrangements on the floor.

Max Mara takes a more literal approach with giant specimen blow-ups of blue and green butterflies. They are used to complement—in an analogous harmony—the yellow coat. Additional solid colored panels of pale yellow, green and blue fill out the window space.

MAX MARA, Madison Ave., New York, NY

CECILE, (FAR LEFT AND LEFT)
Hamilton, Bermuda
Visuals Director: Keith Madieros

EATON'S, Toronto, ON
Div. Manager of Visual
Presentation: Eric Woodward
Photographer: Guntar Kravis

For a sharp contrast nothing does it like Black & White and nothing seems to say black and white better than photography—black and white photography of course.

Eaton's black and white promotion is set in a gallery where the framed and matted black and white photos further play up the Kenneth Cole fashions and fashion trends. The corner presentation adds a dynamic feeling to something that would otherwise be quite passive.

With a salute to Audrey Hepburn and a "Back to the Past" blast, Aston & Gunn combines the classic "little black dress" with black and white photos and some chess pieces—all with a strong retro reference. The black glasses further enhance the Audrey Hepburn theme.

ASTON & GUNN, Bermuda
Visual Presentation Manager: Keith Madieros
Display: Sarah Whitehead

SAKS FIFTH AVENUE, New York, NY
VP of Visual Merchandising: Ken Smart
Dir. of Window Visuals: Randy Yaw

Saks Fifth Avenue creates a vivid impression in sharp black and white with the white back wall patterned with black squares. Assorted larger black squares are randomly laid on the white floor. The garments, on white abstracts, are black and white with a single accent; the red tie with the black suit.

The black and white print gown on the realistic mannequin in the Pilar Rossi, open back window is accompanied by a wrought iron stand topped with an open work urn filled with white snowballs. The mannequin stands on a pewter colored floor mat which complements the silvery pull-down grille.

PILAR ROSSI, Madison Ave., New York, NY
Display Designer: Marc Manigault

BERGDORF GOODMAN,
Fifth Ave., New York, NY
VP of Visual Presentation:
Linda Fargo
Window Presentation
Manager: David Hoey

Bergdorf Goodman's bridal display comes alive in glorious black and white; she's in white and he's in black. What really does it are the photos—blown-up on the black wall and "attached" with the stickum corners we remember from old photo albums. Adding to the scene is the camera on a tripod and the white light reflector.

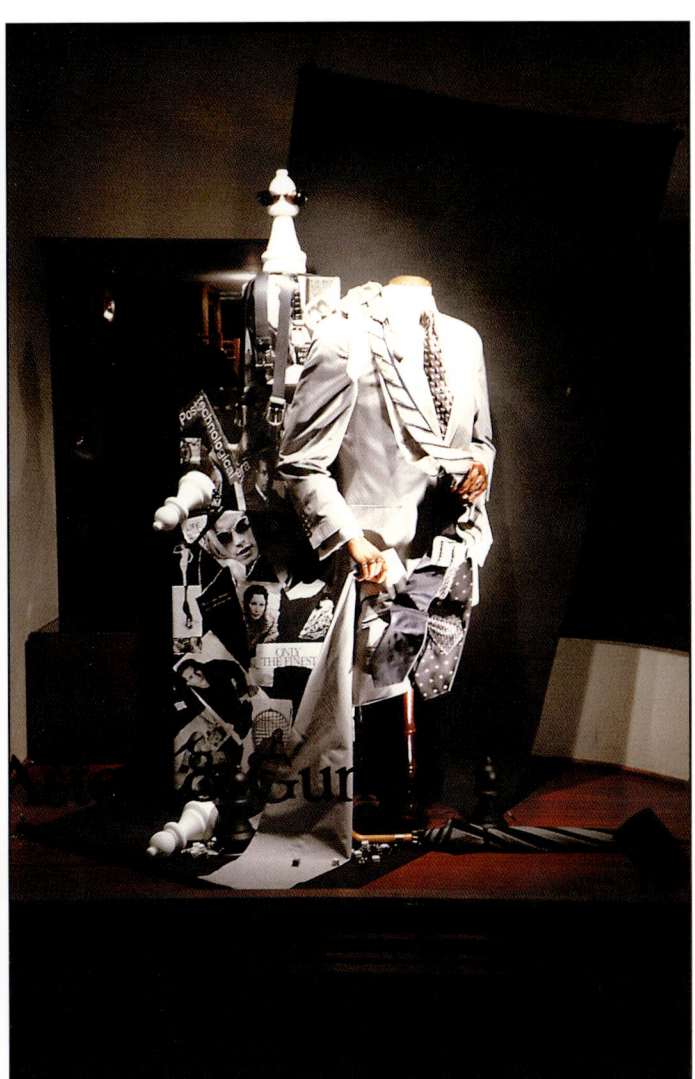

ASTON & GUNN, Bermuda
Visual Presentation Manager: Keith Madieros
Display: Sarah Whitehead

BURBERRYS: E. 57th St., New York, NY
VP of Store VM: Diane Gatterdam

DOLCE & GABBANA, Madison Ave., New York, NY

Black and white Burberry suits are shown in an all-white volume. The vertical metal poles and the hardware are painted white and they support the photo enlargements of the Burberry fashion photography—in black and white.

Another Aston & Gunn black and white window is shown here with a different collage of photography. Here the chess pieces are more important to the composition.

How minimal can you get? Dolce & Gabbana must be the most minimal of minimalists—especially in black and white. Two silvery rods with disk shelves on top support the shoe and bag that accessorize the fur trimmed gown on the form.

MARSHALL FIELD, State St., Chicago, IL
Visual Director, State St.: Amy Meadows

At Marshall Field, in Chicago, they left the chests and chiffoniers somewhere else and just brought in a pile of drawers that are stacked with fashion accessories and coordinates. The drawers are papered with brown corrugated board as are the neckplates of the suit forms. The background is an empire drape of wide, natural muslin.

Bergdorf's Store for Men brings the chest into the window and rather than pull out and stuff the drawers, the chest becomes an interesting prop and also an elevation for the shirt and tie on top.

Chests, drawer units and trunks all add to the clutter of props in this Barneys made-to-order clothing display. Refer to "A Man's World" for other displays like this—a la Barney.

For the display of small jewelry, Peter Rank has used a miniature chest with drawers pulled out from which to drape the Cada gold chains. The chest is covered with gray flannel (or felt) and patches of the same material are applied like "drawers" on the rear unit to show off the earrings.

BERGDORF'S STORE FOR MEN, Fifth Ave., New York, NY
Dir. of V.M., Men's Store: Harry Bader

BOXES & DRAWERS 27

CADA, Munich, Germany
Design: Peter Rank, Deko Rank

BARNEYS, Madison Ave., New York, NY
Creative Director: Simon Doonan
Sr. V.P. Creative Services: David New
V.P. Creative Services: Adamo Di Gregorio

**BURBERRY, (ABOVE AND LEFT) E.57th St., New York, NY
VP Store Design & VM: Diane Gattersdeam**

Burberry is the Burberry plaid; camel, white, black and red! You don't have to say "Burberry" the plaid itself speaks for the name and creates the brand image.

Shown here are several image building, brand promoting displays created by Burberry's display team. Though other plaids and patterns may also be featured—it is their "logo plaid" that always gets the big show in Burberry's windows.

BRANDING BURBERRY 29

BURBERRY, (ABOVE AND RIGHT) E.57th St., New York, NY
VP Store Design & VM: Diane Gattersdeam

**LIBERTY OF LONDON, (ABOVE AND LEFT) Regent St., London
Creative Director: Paul Muller**

Stretchy, almost clear but still quite see-through, on the roll cellophane or food wrap can be used to create the illusion of ice, sleet, of rain or just shimmer and shine.

At Liberty of London, the clear cellophane is stretched across the front glass with just enough ripple left to add a shiny haze to the garments viewed behind. The trick is to get just enough light to bounce off of the stretched material to create the desired illusion.

CELLOPHANE   31

SAKS FIFTH AVE., New York, NY
VP of V.M.: Ken Smart
Window Director: Randy Yaw

HENRI BENDEL, Fifth Ave., New York, NY
Dir. of Visual Presentation: Graham Belman

At Saks, a curtain of clear, clingy acetate or cellophane is set behind the dress forms and just in front of the light trough cut into the floor near the back wall. The blue lights, in the trough, provide the shimmer and shine on the acetate.

Bendel stretches yards and yards of yellow and blue cellophane in their tall, open-back windows. The swirl of the blue brings the viewers eye to the mannequin in the yellow gown while the yellow panels of the shiny stuff back up the blue shoes on the floor.

BIRKS JEWELERS, Montreal, QC
Design & Concept: Lucy-Ann Bouwman
Installation: Lucy-Ann Bouwman/Melanie Girdwood/Keely Meadus
Photographer: Massimo

Children's toys and games are always fair game for a displayperson in need of a prop but no one has gone into these as cleverly nor executed them as beautifully as Lucy Ann Bouwman who did these Birks Jewelry windows. These imaginative settings were produced to showcase the company's fine jewelry, watches and giftware.

Limited to Tiffany-like shadow boxes, Ms. Bouwman constructed the attention getting units. There is the train that passes through a trestle as it moves on a track of rectangular blocks. Highlighted are the two, train stopping gold watches that are resting on triangular blocks so viewers can appreciate the watch faces.

Set within a fantasy facade of arched openings and dramatically raised up from the floor are some exquisite crystal wine glasses. As in the train set-up, the pin-pointed light makes the difference.

Another, art deco-like in design, sets the stage for the diva, show stopping gold necklace in the spotlight on the Ziegfeld stairway. And you always thought these blocks were for children!!

CHILD'S PLAY 33

BIRKS JEWELERS, (RIGHT AND BELOW), Montreal, QC
Design & Concept: Lucy-Ann Bouwman
Installation: Lucy-Ann Bouwman/
Melanie Girdwood/Keely Meadus
Photographer: Massimo

MACY'S, Herald Square, New York, NY
Window Visuals Director: Sam C. Joseph
Sr. Executive Windows/VM: Gil Croy
Photographer: James Mulea

It takes COLOR + LIGHT to really get attention on the street. Here are some color saturated displays—beautifully lit and monochromatic for even greater impact.

RED is always an attention getter and here are three redder than red displays. Macy's did a series of "color themed" windows (another in the set follows) and in this one the hot pink background is flooded with red light. The abstract white mannequins are dressed in garments of the same flaming color. The containers brimming over with red; red flowers tie in with the "dictionary definition" that is boldly printed across the front glass.

Hermes' big red dot on the flat white wall makes a strong focal point while enriching the redness of the hanging leather coat. Balancing the off-center garment are some red strings that end up with red glass tear drops. The white wall contrasts with the red floor pads that further promote the red message.

HERMES, E. 57th St., New York, NY
Display Director: Eric Werner

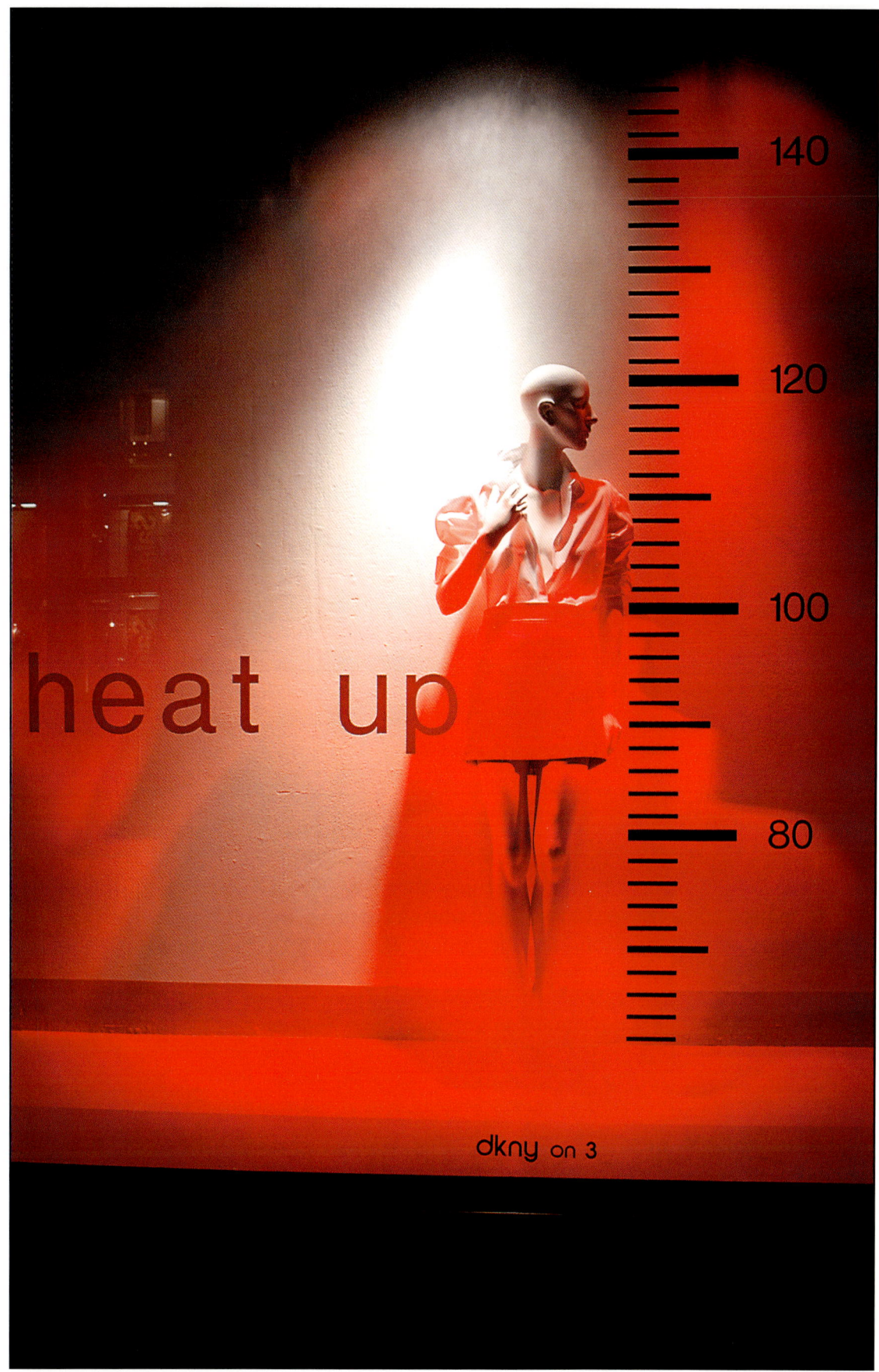

BLOOMINGDALES, Lexington Ave. New York, NY
VP of Visual Merchandising: Jack Hruska
Creative Director: Mike Fisher
Window Manager: Harry Medina

Things are really heating up at Bloomingdales. The temperature is rising as the red light floods the red floor and the red skirt of the white abstract mannequin. To make sure that the viewer gets the point, the thermometer on the right marks up the fashion heat wave.

36 STORE WINDOWS No. 12

BERGDORF GOODMAN, Fifth Ave., New York, NY
VP of Visual Presentation: Linda Fargo
Director of Visual Presentation: David Hoey

Cooling off—with blues and greens! Bergdorf Goodman cools things off for the blue outfit on the white abstract with the medium blue background and the appointment sheets with dates and times in pale aqua. The latter fill out the cool blue illuminated space and suggest that this outfit can go almost anywhere-anytime.

The Bally "B" becomes a strong graphic image in the monochromatic green window that features mostly white fashion accessories. It is the calming, soothing green color that reaches out and then steps back to become the contrasting background for the white products that move into prominence.

BALLY'S, Fifth Ave., New York, NY

GUCCI, Fifth Ave., New York, NY
Corporate Director of Visual Presentation: James Knight

Another Macy's window setting—this time in monochromatic blue. It follows the same format as the red one previously shown except it is the striking contrast from colored window to window that made the series so very effective-and striking.

Gucci's soft, gentle rose-beige coat is promoted by the assorted rectangular forms that repeat in the background in the same soft color. The rear wall is a deeper shade of the warm neutral, and pink lights add the pleasant glow that fills the space and accentuates the garment.

MACY'S, Herald Square, New York, NY
Window Visuals Director: Sam C. Joseph
Sr. Executive Windows/VM: Gil Croy
Photographer: James Mulea

Circles and cylinders of bright, sharp colors polka-dot the rear, white wall and serve as accents and risers on the equally white floor of the Saks Fifth Ave. window. The display promotes Cynthia Rowley handbags which are presented atop the cylinders centered in the window. Though most of the fashions are in tints and shades of red, the elevated abstract mannequin wears a print dress that is filled with the colors used for the window and floor accents.

In another Saks display there are horizontal bands across part of the rear wall and colored cubes are set down on the rose colored floor. More squares in pink, lavender and apricot balance the horizontal bands of similar colors on the lavender tinted rear wall.

SAKS FIFTH AVE., (ABOVE AND RIGHT) **New York, NY**
VP of Visual Merchandising: Ken Smart
Window Visuals Director: Randy Yaw

COLOR + FORM   39

FERREGAMO, Fifth Ave., New York, NY
Director of Visuals: John Krenek

MAX MARA, Madison Ave., New York, NY

Max Mara plays up a series of dynamic angular forms in yellow, red and blue against a simple rectangle of deeper blue that serves as a background in this open back window. A shiny, chrome yellow floor pad pulls it all together to create a "directional" composition that leads the viewer's eye to the costume on the headless form.

Ferregamo's bag and shoe display features a strong, silver-framed panel of wood stained red set against a yellow wall. The shoes and bags are highlighted on orange squares that rest on the green stained table.

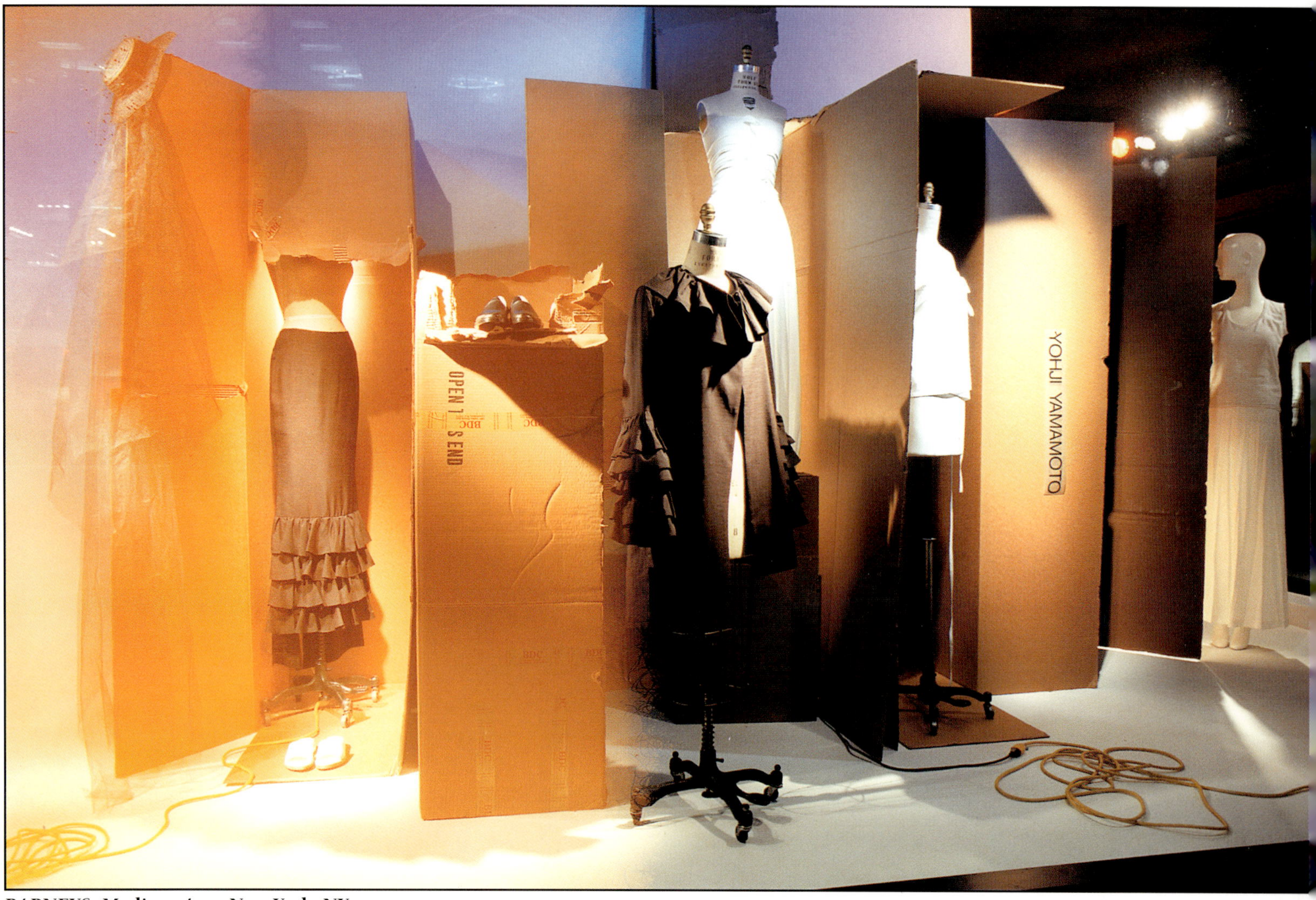

BARNEYS, Madison Ave., New York, NY
Creative Director: Simon Doonan
Sr. V.P. Creative Services: David New
V.P. Creative Services: Adamo Di Gregorio

This very inexpensive material—corrugated board—is a most versatile display material. It is rigid enough to stand on its own or even support weight, it is easy to curve, swirl and bend and it is often retrieved from the trash where old cartons are tossed.

Barneys puts the corrugated board to its traditional use. The giant cartons—maybe old or maybe made to look old and pre-used—reveal some "new arrivals": The "just in" garments appear on dress forms and headless figures that appear to have been packed up in these cartons. Note how some have been "worn" and "torn" by someone who couldn't wait to see what was inside. A great concept for introducing a new season—a new line—or new imports.

In the Cada display window we get the shipping cartons in miniature for the show of jewelry. The boxes are divided into small cases and Cada is stenciled on the back of the carton.

CADA, Munich, Germany
Design: Peter Rank, Deko Rank

CORRUGATED BOARD 41

HENRI BENDEL, Fifth Ave., New York, NY
Display Director: Graham Belman

Henri Bendel makes use of the neutral colored but patterned material to create a series of geometric forms to complement the gray garments worn by the abstract mannequins in the open back window. Note how the forms all accentuate the vertical line thus adding visual prestige to the clothing. In another Bendel window the rolling corrugated material creates a landscape of hills, mountains and what could even be a full moon. The undulating, curving lines are finished with wavelike tops to further suggest softness and femininity.

CARSON PIRIE SCOTT, State St., Chicago, IL
V.P. of V.M.: Rick Schlenther
Reg. V.M. Dir.: Ted Georgiou

For the TUBU display of streetwear for young men, the denim outfits are shown against oil cans, traffic signs and warning lights that are all part of the urban streetscape. In the blacked out window, the very clean and orderly look contrasts with the "let it all hang out" attitude of the clothes.

Levi's blue denims and the colored denims of Marithe & Francois Girbaud get a "hang up" presentation in the Carson Pirie Scott windows. A mahogany colored panel serves as a background and the assorted pieces of clothing are suspended down and hung off a variety of belts. Not only is this an effective way to display shorts—at eye level—it also makes a great point of promoting the belts as a fashion accessory.

Palais Royale takes a western spin on blue jeans— also complemented with red. Particularly interesting is the modern, urban interpretation of the corrugated cacti that set the scene. Note the use of small red lights to serve as the thorny prickles that accentuate the cacti plants. A skull suggests the desert which is represented by a puddle of sand.

PALAIS ROYALE, Houston, TX

CARSON PIRIE SCOTT, (ABOVE AND BELOW) **State St., Chicago, IL**
V.P. of V.M.: Rick Schlenther
Reg. V.M. Dir.: Ted Georgiou

ZCMI, (ABOVE AND RIGHT) **Salt Lake City, UT**
Visuals Director: Mike Stevens
Design: Diane Call & Monte Blunk

How can you love someone who doesn't love dogs? Doggone it! A dog—like a baby—will always do it. It is a Pavlovian reaction: show a dog in the window and watch people "oh!" and "ah!" over it. If you can't get "housebroken" ones—or well trained ones—there are always the replicas as you can see here.

At ZCMI the cartoony dog was added to complete the "Our Gang" look that showed off children's summer fun wear. An RCA kind of dog does duty watching the whimsical mobile that flashes the sparkling jewelry created by St. John.

Bergdorf's Store for Men introduced "Blue Dog" as dad's friend. In addition to the framed prints of Blue Dog, dad gets to walk a cut-out version of the popular dog. The blue hydrant is a nice touch and adds another dollop of humor to this Father's Day promotion.

A collection of period hunting dog prints plus some pieces of sculpture set the scene for the tweedy men with their dog-headed walking sticks in Saks window. A touch of British class.

For Nymphenburg Porzellan, Peter Rank showed off the store's collection of porcelain and china dogs. An all-white mannequin is taking them out for an airing and the wonderful collection is tied together with white ribbon leashes.

DOGGIE IN THE WINDOW 45

NYMPHENBURG PORZELLAN, Munich, Germany
Design: Peter Rank, Deko Rank

BERGDORF, STORE FOR MEN: Fifth Ave., New York, NY
Dir. of V.M. Men's Store: Harry Bader

SAKS FIFTH AVE., New York, NY
V.P. of V. M. Ken Smart
Dir. of Windows: Randy Yaw

ERMENEGILDO ZEGNA, Fifth Ave., New York, NY
VM Director: Mark Hoch

BARNEYS, Madison Ave., New York, NY
Sr. Creative Director: Simon Doonan
Sr. VP Creative Services: David New
VP Creative Services: Adamo DiGregorio

Who can resist the "doggie-in-the-window" whether the doggie is stuffed, shellacked, cut-out and colored—or just photographed over and over and over again. Sometimes you don't even need to see the doggie to know that it is somewhere near.

At Zegna, the headless forms in white are out for an airing and a cut-out dog has come along to help set the scene. Behind the simple white frame is a blow up of the Zegna man—in full color. The print serves as a divider in the open-back window.

Barneys salutes "Sweetie"—a poster and "cover" dog. Adding to the humor of the presentation is the trail of dog food pellets making a circuitous route through the all white setting, the paw prints, and the dozens and dozens of pictures of Sweetie. Viewed on the right is a fashion presentation in this setting.

In much the same vein are the Birks and Macy's windows. The Macy back wall has a giant dog bone formed out of hundreds of actual dog bone biscuits. Artfully painted dogs, on leashes, accompany the realistic mannequins in their colorfully patterned dresses.

Birks makes a big deal out of their canvas "doggie bags" and also fill an elegant silver bowl with dog biscuits. Note the beautiful silver dogs resting in the foreground. The frosted plaque carries the "doggie" message.

DOG-GONE! 47

MACY'S, Herald Square, New York, NY
Window Director: Sam Joseph

THE BOOK STORE, Madison Ave.
New York, NY

BIRKS, Montreal, Canada
Visuals Director: Lucy Anne Bouwman
Photographer: Massimo

TIFFANY, Fifth Ave., New York, NY
Visual Director: Robert Rufino

Where would Easter be or how would we know it was Easter without eggs? Pastel tinted, hand dipped, painted or appliqued and even egg-facsimiles—anything goes. Tiffany added a "light" touch with egg shaped akari lanterns dripping gold ribbons. They are suspended in a window glowing with golden light. On the floor pad—some eggs—one cracked. Spilling forth are some gold trinkets a la Tiffany.

Cada, in Munich, relied on gold foil wrapped chocolate eggs—encased in miniature wooden crates—to promote their jewelry for Easter. The even smaller wood crates are used to show off some of the selected pieces.

CADA, Munich, Germany
Design & Execution:
Peter Rank, Deko Rank

TIFFANY, (LEFT AND BELOW)
Munich, Germany
**Design & Execution:
Peter Rank, Deko Rank**

Tiffany in Munich featured ostrich sized eggs in their cool blue-lit windows. Rough woven wicker baskets become nests to hold the eggs. In one window the big egg is cracked open to reveal a collection of the familiar pale blue Tiffany gift boxes plus some smaller, regular size eggs. In still another a feathered chick sits atop the giant egg and it holds a gold chain like an oversized worm. More gold jewelry is shown in the nest snuggled up to the regular eggs.

SAKS FIFTH AVE., Fifth Ave., New York, NY
VP of Visual Merchandising: Ken Smart
Window Visual Director: Randy Yaw

Taking the "usual" and turning it into the "unusual" is what display is all about. It isn't about how much one spends to get something rare and unique to show as a prop or as part of a setting but how to take everyday things that we encounter in passing and turn them—by display magic and imagination—into arresting things that we stop to look at, as if for the first time.

Saks has fun with our preoccupation with dieting, exercising and re-shaping our shapes. Using machines usually found in gyms and work-out spots and when we are in sweats or shorts, the display people have moved them into the store's front window and teamed them with realistic mannequins in Marc Jacobs outfits. The red heart candy boxes taunt us even more as do the ribbons of copy on the glass as we quest for slim fast lines.

At Burberry's, the display team presents a busy day in a working man's schedule. At 7:30 AM it is time to "Fluff & Fold" as we dress for the occasion. The familiar ironing board is backed up by signature Burberry plaid ironing board covers which are not so ordinary. Atop the ironing board a Burberry plaid shirt is getting the fluff and fold treatment. At 2:15 PM it is time for a water cooler break and to pick up some inter-office gossip. The water cooler creates the setting while the pattern of desk pad calendars on the wall suggest the location.

EVERYDAY OBJECTS   51

BURBERRYS, (ABOVE AND RIGHT) E. 57th St., New York, NY
VP Store Design & Visual Merchandising: Diane Gatterdam

BERGDORF GOODMAN, Fifth Ave., New York, NY
VP of Visual Merchandising: Linda Fargo
Window Director: David Hoey

Bergdorf takes something quite ordinary and a few less ordinary objects to create fun settings in the windows. I'm sure it isn't everyday we get to see a prison cell or a safe being "blown" but we certainly have seen them in movies and on TV. Here they create a truly "arresting" setting for fashionable wear. The sticks of dynamite, the money bags, and the tintype on the wall all add humor—and a sense of recognition—to the display.

EVERYDAY OBJECTS

Not every one gets to see anatomy models and charts everyday but we recognize them—we know them—and certainly don't expect to see them in a display window. The designers have added scales, beakers, Bunsen burners and other lab paraphernalia to enhance the science oriented window setting.

Highly reflective, brand new and shiny paint cans and paint pans create a sparkling and shimmering background for the men's suits in Bergdorf's Store for Men window. There are also reflector lamps and other equally shiny objects in the dimensional montage that only proves that familiarity doesn't necessarily breed contempt but can inspire a shopping spree.

BERGDORF GOODMAN,
(ABOVE AND LEFT)
Fifth Ave., New York, NY
VP of Visual Merchandising:
Linda Fargo
Window Director: David Hoey

TIFFANY, (ABOVE AND RIGHT), Munich, Germany
Peter Rank of Deko Rank

Peter Rank of Deko Rank of Munich, has mastered the art of shadow box display and here are some of his creations using everyday objects.

It is picnic time at Tiffany's in Munich, so Rank has the soda cooled and the griddle hot. Green fabrics, grass matting and plastic sheeting are combined with the everyday objects that are used here to hold and show the jewelry.

At Sevigne, Rank raids the kitchen for his props to add fun and interest to the costume jewelry being featured. Cookie sheets, stainless steel ladles and spoons, colanders and sieves, pots and pans—with additions of marabou and feathery fluff are all it takes. What's cooking? Sevigne's windows and the merchandise on display.

EVERYDAY OBJECTS 55

SEVIGNE, (ALL) Munich, Germany
Peter Rank of Deko Rank

BERGDORF GOODMAN, Fifth Ave., New York, NY
VP of Visual Merchandising: Linda Fargo
Window Director: David Hoey

The colors are changing as the seasons change. New colors, new looks, new styles, new accessories to brighten up last year's purchases. It's time for rough textures, earthy colors and warm glowing lights.

At Bergdorf's the background is a three dimensional collage of branches, twigs, spirals of birch bark, dried leaves and photos of birds torn out of some old ornithology books. The realistic mannequins are set off-center and balanced by the fall foliage in the background. The warm light enriches the textures of the varied textured materials.

Burberry's combines branches of birch with weathered planks of rough-sawn wood to create a seasonal/lifestyle setting for the two, stylized male figures. Note the curled, stripped birch bark lying on the stained, rough wood planked floor.

To frame the "Maid of Gold" outfit by Stephen Sprouse, the display people at Bloomingdale's have created a dramatic framework of rough branches bound with burlap webbing. It could be a stylized tepee—or a series of natural step-ladders in forced perspective. With the warm shower of golden light it becomes a truly dramatic setting for a one-of-a-kind presentation.

BURBERRY'S, E. 57th St., New York, NY
VP Store Design & V. M.: Diane Gatterdam

BLOOMINGDALES, Lexington Ave., New York, NY
VP of Visual Merchandising: Jack Hruska
Creative Director: Mike Fisher
Window Manager: Harry Medina

At Holland & Holland the country dressing gets a countrified setting that combines giant color photo blow-ups with natural elements such as branches, twigs, and dried foliage. Since these are open back windows, the 4 ft. x 8 ft. background panels separate the featured garments realistically displayed on dress and suit forms from the actual store beyond. The floor is flooded with a vast assortment of "go-with" accessories.

HOLLAND & HOLLAND
(ABOVE AND RIGHT)
E. 57th St., New York, NY

BARNEYS, Madison Ave., New York, NY
Creative Director: Simon Doonan
Sr. VP, Creative Services: David New
VP, Creative Services: Adamo DiGregorio

BURBERRY'S, E.57th St., New York, NY
VP of Visual Merchandising
& Store Design: Diane Gatterdam

Burberry's plays up their signature Burberry plaid in the shadowy, illusionary setting of bare, bare branches and "water-color" trees. The egg-heads on the dress forms figures add to the surreal quality of the presentation. The eerie lighting does manage to play up the neutral coats while accenting the famous plaid trim.

The sole figure in Barney's window is not Joan of Arc about to be burned at the stake but the pile-up of dried branches, twigs and leaves could have been used back then. The blue sky background complements the warm light on the yellow/gold coat while the proposed fashion accessories are tossed in amid the fagots.

SAKS FIFTH AVE., (LEFT AND BELOW) New York, NY
VP of VM: Ken Smart
Window Visual Director: Randy Yaw

Fall arrives in a flurry of flaming foliage; reds, golds, and rich, rich earthy colors. Fashions usually take on the same vibrant colors and the terra cottas, browns and beiges enrich the window scene.

At Saks Fifth Ave. it is a sweep of fall foliage that starts with the special bamboo pronged rakes used to gather up the leaves that have fallen and it ends up with wheelbarrows filled to overflowing with the colorful leaves—and the fashion accessories. The displaypersons have taken "creative liberties" with these mundane, everyday, usually locked-in-a-garage props to create arresting displays on the very urban and sophisticated Fifth Ave. in New York City. Rich, red lighting and the red orange floor pads add to the color of the season.

FALL 61

MISS JACKSON'S, (ALL) Tulsa, OK
Creative Director: Betty Batey

Miss Jackson's, an exclusive women's fashion shop in Tulsa, OK, welcomed fall with fall foliage. In addition to the mannequins that were completely shingled over with thousands of artificial leaves of myriad colors, some of the mannequins used to show off the very upscale fashions were treated to elaborate hairdos constructed of preserved fall leaves. The clothes being featured were all rich, and earthy in color. Expert lighting played up what really mattered.

MACY'S, Herald Square, New York, NY
VP, Director of Visual
Merchandising: Mark Minichiello
Director of Windows: Sam C. Joseph
3D Figures: Creative Arts,
Pinellas Park, FL
Lighting Design: Douglas Fowler
Photography: James Mulea, NY

An annual event that is as much anticipated by New Yorkers as is the Thanksgiving Parade is Macy's spring splash of flowers, shrubs, and sprouting plants at the Flower Show. You know that Spring is here when Macy's opens its front windows that are overflowing with all of that glorious greenery and the riot of familiar and exotic flowers. This year's theme tied in with the wonderful adventures of Winnie the Pooh—thus adding another dimension to the already beckoning windows. The three dimensional figures, created by Creative Arts, moved in and around the technicolor forest of fresh blooms to delight viewers of all ages.

FLOWER SHOW 63

MACY'S, (ALL) Herald Square, New York, NY
VP, Director of Visual Merchandising: Mark Minichiello
Director of Windows: Sam C. Joseph
3D Figures: Creative Arts, Pinellas Park, FL
Lighting Design: Douglas Fowler
Photography: James Mulea, NY

A bit overstated and overblown but these giant spring blossoms have the power to get the message across. Whether the "message" is a new color—a fashion look or just a seasonal one—FLOWER POWER works!

Harrod's, in London, goes all out with exotic flowers blown up to fill up most of the back wall of the window. The clothes being shown are color-keyed to the brilliant blossoms and the Flower Power tattoos, on the arms of the white headless forms, add more impact to the floral story.

HARROD'S, (TOP AND ABOVE) **Knightsbridge, London, UK**
Display Director: Mark Briggs
Display Designer: Sarah Southgate
Photography: Melvyn Vincent

FLOWER POWER 65

FERRAGAMO, (ABOVE AND LEFT) Fifth Ave., New York, NY
Dir. Of Visuals: John Krenek
Asst. Director: Jesse Barber

Photo blow-ups of flowers make brilliant background screens for the Ferragamo fashion accessories shown on the padded dress forms. The strong color of the flower panels is reflected on the slick, white plastic floor boards to completely envelop the dress forms in an aura of that color.

VALENTINO, Fifth Ave., New York, NY
Dir. Of Visuals: Jordi Lopez

ZCMI, Salt Lake City, Utah
Visuals Director: Mike Stephens
Designer: Alysa Revell

Valentino's soaring, two-story window is filled with panels of overstated flower heads contained within black metal framework. The peach-rose and warm blue colors of the flowers are enhanced by the banners of the colors surrounding the screen and together they enrich the pastel-toned merchandise on display on the dress and suit forms.

ZCMI went with "pocket full of posies" for a series of youth oriented Spring windows. Giant tissue flowers in orange, cerise and pink make a striking setting for the elegant dolls shown here raised up on stem-like green platforms.

FLOWER POWER 67

SAKS FIFTH AVE., (ABOVE AND RIGHT) New York, NY
VP of Visual Merchandising: Ken Smart
Window Visual Director: Randy Yaw

Saks Fifth Ave. made some high power, brightly colored flower statements with the windows shown here. With giant yellow suns, overdeveloped, cut-out and brilliantly colored flowers and toadstools popping up from the grass green floor, the color coordinated print outfits stand out from the deep, rich, ultramarine blue background. The flat artwork combined with the stylized mannequins makes for a fun, theatrical feeling.

CHRISTIAN DIOR, Fifth Ave. New York, NY

TIFFANY, Fifth Ave., New York, NY
Visuals Director: Robert Rufino

Bouquets, nosegays, urns filled, vases overflowing, potted in pots—whatever! In Christian Dior's theatrical vignette, a flat cut-out drape hangs against the glass and a paneled wall serves as a background for the evening gowned mannequin. The blue hydrangeas in the black, strap metal urn provides a seasonal touch for the violet gown. Fallen buds are scattered over the green floor and the train of the gown. A lovely example of an analogous harmony in a window setting: green, blue and violet.

Tiffany's brings the flowering plants in their terra cotta clay pots into their shadow box window. Adding to the overall springtime ambiance is the robin's blue eggs in the metal basket, the textured floor, the weather wrought iron chair and the aqua light on the walls.

FLORAL ARRANGEMENTS 69

CECILE, Hamilton, Bermuda
Visual Presentation Director: Keith Madieros
Display: Sandra Whitehead

Cecile in Bermuda plays up the yellow gold floral print of the dess by placing a clump of sunflowers up front. Surrounding flowers and dress are bees—dozens and dozens of them swarming around. The net draped over the hat is a nice accent to play up the part of the bees in the display.

The elegant floral arrangement in Lalique's window only enhances what is already refined and lovely. The casually draped scarf breaks up what could have been a too formal and too aloof look.

LALIQUE, Madison Ave., New York, NY

Shiny! Shiny! Shiny! And even more so when crunched, crinkled and catching lights on the thousands of reflective facets. Whether it is sheets of mylar or off of rolls of household tinfoil wrap or aluminum foil—it is a tricky material that needs to be handled to make it work without overwhelming the merchandise in the display.

Bergdorf has just unwrapped the most delicious "sweets" available. The two realistic mannequins in their shiny and shimmering outfits are surrounded by a giant explosion of crinkled foil—like an unwrapped Hershey's "kiss." The many, many reflective surfaces catch and reflect the lights to create a dazzling, attention getting window display.

At Moschino, the scrunched up silvery "parachutes" carry the Moschino handbags against a cloud filled, silky blue sky.

BERGDORF GOODMAN
Fifth Ave., New York, NY
VP of Visual Presentation: Linda Fargo
Window Director: David Hoey

MOSCHINO, Madison Ave, New York, NY
Display: David Griffin

FOIL-ED AGAIN

BLOOMINGDALE'S, Lexington Ave., New York, NY
VP of V.M.: Jack Hruska
Creative Director: Mike Fischer

It is space-age dynamics at Bloomingdale's where a make believe spaceperson—in a shimmering mylar cover-all—stands guard over a mysterious tank with a coil of pipe going everywhere and nowhere. Not your everyday dance frock!

This upscale men's shop in a Singapore Mall made "pillows" out of the mylar material and tossed them about the shallow window. The background is a cascade of the same, silvery stuff. A very stylish, yet simple, setting.

Men's Shop, Singapore

BARNEYS, Madison Ave., New York, NY
Creative Director: Simon Doonan
Sr. VP of Creative Services: David New
VP of Creative Services: Adamo DiGregorio

What do potatoes have to do with an elegant, silver mesh gown? Not an awful lot! As a matter of fact—nothing at all but sheer contrast. The contrast between the divine designer gown and the lowly, plebian potato; the contrast between the subtle shimmer of the fabric and the matte, earthy color of the spud. The potatoes are casually arranged on the white floor but nailed into clusters on the equally white wall by means of large, silvery accented carpenter's nails.

Tiffany used lemons to accent the pitcher and glasses that would be just right for some upscaled lemonade. Note the yellow and white checkered napkin and the yellow ribbons used to hold the suspended shelf; they further the lemon yellow accent.

Dooney & Burke played the scale game (see OVER-SCALED) to show off their hand crafted leather bags. They are shown alongside giant apples and pears— "the pick of the crop." Ghurka, for its leather goods, resorted to green pears on and off the bough. At eye level the pears are attached to the leafy branch with a handsome leather belt playing the snake in this updated Garden of Eden. Pears are also piled up and spill out of the galvanized pail. The pale yellow tinted floor pad accentuates the fresh green color of the pears which in turn complements the russet tones of the leather goods.

FRUITS & VEGGIES 73

TIFFANY, Manhasset, New York, NY

GHURKA, New York, NY

DOONEY & BURKE, New York, NY

LORD & TAYLOR, (ABOVE AND RIGHT)
Fifth Ave., New York, NY
Creative Director: Manoel Renha

The grass is always greener—especially in windows when Spring is here! Lord & Taylor took their realistic mannequins out into the park to show off their new pastel tinted outfits. A park bench painted white, some gravel artfully arranged to suggest a path, some vines and branches and a painted background to set the time and place: Sunday or any day in the park—with or without George.

Macy's just brought in the grass. Boxes of bright green grass fill up half of the window and the fluorescent fixtures suspended over the boxes provide grow and show light. The daffodil colored suits are shown on dress forms and they are complemented by the yellow green light on the back wall.

Christian Dior's window in Dusseldorf, Germany was highlighted by grass covered, overscaled garden shears and the floor was covered with more of the artificial grass. The flowers are abloom on the Dior outfit and the hat that tops it off.

The Gap, in Chicago, was all ready for spring. The green garden hose was all it took to turn the dress forms lined up in their simple, casual outfits into something special and a call to Springtime action.

GARDENS & GARDENING 75

MACY'S, Herald Square,
New York, NY
VP of VM: Mark
Minichiello
Window Director:
Sam C. Joseph

CHRISTIAN DIOR, Dusseldorf, Germany

THE GAP, Michigan Ave., Chicago, IL

BERGDORF GOODMAN, Fifth Ave., New York, NY
V.P. of Visual Presentation: Linda Fargo
Assoc. Creative Director: David Hoey

Gray may be a shadow color somewhere between the extremes of black and white but gray is also coming out of the shadows as a fashion statement color. For those who are tired of black and never quite tuned in on brown this very neutral, goes-with-everything and at any time color, now steps into its own.

Bergdorf plays the neutrality of gray with the bright accent color of red in the background and on the props all to reinforce the thin red line that runs down the pant leg of the featured garment. The white sweater helps to enliven the gray.

Ferregamo's display salutes the total neutrality of gray and the fashion forward statement of the white pin striped fabric. The well suited, headless form stands beside an almost invisible clear plastic chair upon which rests a white bag. The chrome outline screen provides a back-up for the form and restates the vertical line of the pose and the pinstripe pattern.

SALVATORE FERREGAMO, Fifth Ave., New York, NY
Dir. of Visuals: John Krenek
Asst. Dir.: Jesse Barber

T. EATON, Toronto, ON, Canada
Div. Mgr. of V.M. Presentation: Eric Woodward
Visual Mgr.: Sonia Hamori
Photographer: Guntar Kravis

T. Eaton's gray promotion is a monochromatic study of grays that lead to the black accents of the bag, the hosiery and the shoes. The soft gray background is accented with three deeper gray squares that effectively balance and complement the realistic mannequin—in the light—in the foreground.

Like an old '30s or '40s film noir movie, everything is black and white—but ends up as a palette of grays. Gianfranco Ferre's window features a variety of gray prints and patterns against the silvery pattern of the venetian blinds. Black and white accessories are visible on the floor in the foreground.

GIANFRANCO FERRE, Madison Ave., New York, NY
Display: Marc Manigault

BLOOMINGDALE'S, Lexington Ave., New York, NY
Sr. VP of VM: Jack Hruska
VP of VM: Rachel Arnold
Dir. of Stores, VM: Eleanor Smith

What used to be a time for kids to paint their faces, dress up in discarded old clothes or home-made costumes has now been taken over by Generation X and Y and is celebrated with parties and parades. It is no longer just for the kiddies!

The little black dress was never more witchy or bewitching than the one that was worn by the realistic mannequin in Bloomingdale's window. The little, black Balmain velvet dress is accompanied by a line-up of black cats—one of Halloween's favorite symbols. Note the balls of black yarn on the far right and how the yarn is threaded through the mannequin's hand and then on the kittens—to tie the composition together and lead the viewer's eye.

More cats! Lord & Taylor subtly acknowledges the circled date on the October calendar with the back-lit panel featuring the playful black cats while a dimensional one—on the floor—on the right—is highlighted with a red-orange glow. It continues the motif behind the fashions being offered while also saluting a popular holiday.

Swatch goes right to the graveyard for their Halloween setting with skeleton-puppets, bats, graves and tombstones. Eerie, spooky but fun!! Note how even the skeletons have their Swatch watches—in the pinpoints of light—to add some color to their otherwise lifeless existence.

HALLOWEEN 79

LORD & TAYLOR, New York, NY
Creative Director: Manoel Renha
Designer: Jan Topercer

SWATCH, New York, NY

BERGDORF GOODMAN, Fifth Ave., New York, NY
VP of Visual Presentation: Linda Fargo
Window Visual Director: David Hoey

Whether it is hemlines or designer lines—they make fashion headlines. Magazines and newspapers are always vehicles for getting the message across and they are even more successful at doing the job when they are used in the window with the merchandise.

Bergdorf moved their mannequins out into the street and recreated the illusion of a streetcorner newsstand/kiosk to tell their fashion story. The background and the floor are all artworked on a roll of seamless paper that unrolls off the rear wall of the window—behind the two very stylized mannequins. The magazines and newspapers are sketchily rendered and an old wire newspaper stand—just behind the mannequin in black—carries actual newspaper-in French—of course!!

Barneys sets the record straight and also the tone for their Giorgio Armani collection of menswear with a background made up of row upon row of rolled up Wall Street Journals. Note how the papers are alternated to add interest and create a more interesting pattern on the rear wall.

Macy's makes the news. The background is a collage of blow-ups of want ads in black and white and actual newspapers are stacked around the mannequin. She is dressed and ready to make it in the "asphalt jungle" with her zebra striped top and undaunted red skirt. The red bag and the faux leopard patterned one are resting atop the piled up newspapers. Not only is this a brilliant play of word and image; the black and white "in print" makes a great foil for the red accented merchandise.

IN PRINT 81

MACY'S, Herald Square, New York, NY
VP of VM: Marc Minichiello
Window Visual Director: Sam Joseph
Sr. Exec of Windows: Gil Croy

BARNEYS, Madison Ave., New York, NY
Creative Director: Simon Doonan
Sr.VP of Creative Services: David New
VP of Creative Services: Adamo DiGregorio

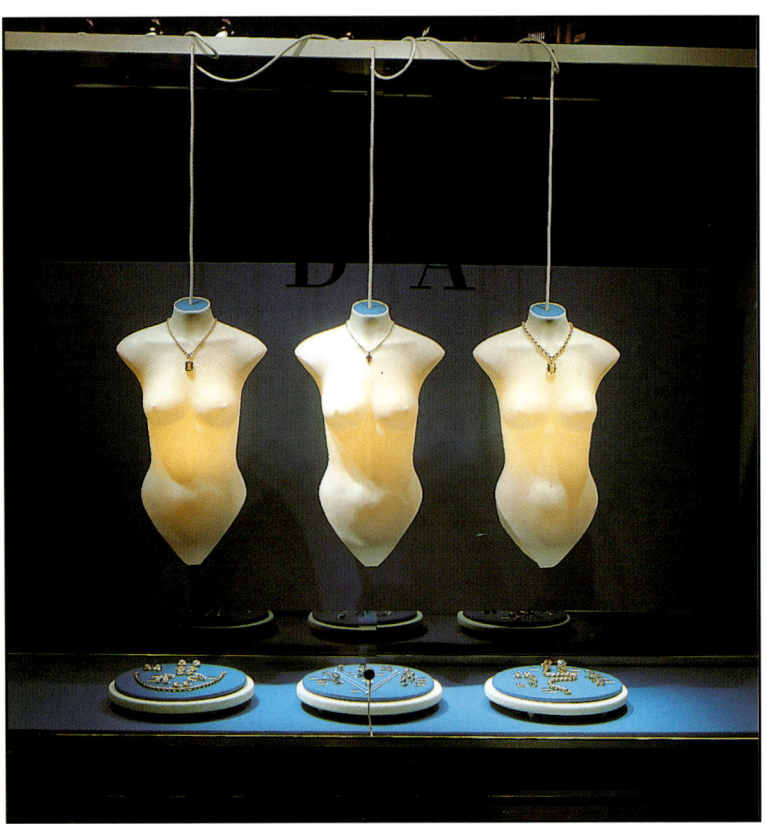

CADA, Munich, Germany
Peter Rank at Deko Rank

Let there be light! Lots of light! Let there be lamps to highlight and create shadows—that drop down or stand up and make illuminating statements. Let there be light to paint the walls with color or gobos to add floating patterns and shapes. Let there be back-lit, front-lit—let there be highlights and low-lights. To catch the viewer's eye—there must be light!

Lamp lights and bulbs add light and luster to these displays. At ZCMI, the "Ultra Violet Eyewear" promotion calls for ultra violet light or at least myriad bare bulbs in many colors to illuminate the sunglasses in the small window. The strong, brightly colored clothes alone would call for sunglasses.

At Cada, translucent miniature body forms are turned into hanging lamps over the display pads on which the jewelry is displayed. The forms also wear some of the featured items.

ZCMI, Salt Lake City, Utah
Mike Stevens: Display Director

LORD & TAYLOR, Fifth Ave., New York, NY
VP of Visual Merchandising: Cal Partridge
Creative Director: Manoel Renha

In a more romantic mood, Lord & Taylor drops crystal shaded bulbs surrounded by prisms over the be-gowned mannequins in the stylized garden setting. More sparkly crystals fill the two screens that frame the scene.

A small, turning signal lamp on a pedestal in Bloomingdale's window does a big job of painting the rear wall with sunlight and moonlight. The yellow and blue colors wash over the rear wall with the torn paper collage that suggests a city skyline.

BLOOMINGDALES, Lexington Ave., New York, NY
VP of Visual Merchandising: Jack Hruska
Creative Director: Mike Fisher
Window Manager: Harry Medina

MARSHALL FIELD, State St., Chicago, IL.
VP of Visual Merchandising for Dayton-Hudson: Jamie Becker
Window Director, State St.: Amy Fisher
Photographer: Susan Kezon

Marshall Field salutes "After Hours" with reflective cylinders in the rear and hanging bare bulbs descending over a group all dressed up to go out on the town. Adding to the "let's dance" attitude are the floating gobo lights on the pink walls—like the lights that flash off of and reflect anywhere when the disco ball is turning. It is definitely Party Time done simply and tastefully.

Light paints the walls and adds mystery and movement to the Bloomingdales displays that feature realistic mannequins in gowns. Streaks of paint are splashed across the front glass and on the rear wall to further enhance the "art work" of the light patterns moving across the rear walls.

LIGHTS 'N' LAMPS   85

BLOOMINGDALES, (ABOVE AND LEFT)
Lexington Ave., New York, NY
VP of Visual Merchandising: Jack Hruska
Creative Director: Mike Fisher
Window Manager: Harry Medina

HENRI BENDEL, Fifth Ave., New York, NY
Dir. of Visual Presentation: Graham Belman

All sorts of novelty and decorative lights and lighting techniques can be adapted to window and interior displays from LED electronic bands as shown beneath the Henri Bendel display of Trish McEvoy clothes to the sparkle and shine of fiberoptics in the black panel behind the glitter topped black gown in the St. John's window. The Trish McEvoy designer/brand name gains even more in importance in the red streamer of light sign that carries the message below the display than from the lettered background panel in the window. The glitter of colors in the St. John gown gets a bigger replay in the fiberoptics on the panel that serves as the background.

ST. JOHN BOUTIQUE, Fifth Ave., New York, NY
Creative Director: Kelly Gray

LIGHTS 'N' LAMPS 87

GUCCI, Fifth Ave., New York, NY
Corp. Dir. of Visual Presentation:
James Knight

ST. JOHN BOUTIQUE, Fifth Ave., New York, NY
Creative Director: Kelly Gray

In another display at St. John, colored gels are used to create the multi-colored star pattern on the white panel. The gels fill the circular openings cut in the 4 ft. x 8 ft. foam board panel which is illuminated from behind so the colors truly glow. Gucci also uses a back-lit panel to play up the importance of the suit's silhouette only here the translucent material has a pattern on it for greater interest and also to soften the overall effect.

BERGDORF GOODMAN, Fifth Ave., New York, NY
VP of Visual Presentation: **Linda Fargo**
Window Visual Dir.: **David Hoey**

Right out of the lumber yard; raw, natural unfinished and unstained. Slats, boards, beams, joists and other natural wood building materials become creative elements in the hands of talented displaypersons.

To feature the natural, pale honey-toned fashions, the design team at Bergdorf's created this giant "sculpture" of wood slats and lathe strips that dominates center stage in the window. It is accented with fashion accessories as well as bits and pieces of other natural and neutral textured materials such as corrugated board, crumpled kraft paper, bits of bark and burlap. The slats are set out helter-skelter on the white floor to repeat the motif of the 3D central prop.

In contrast, Macy's designers used 4x4s with nickel plated angle joints to affect the dynamic "check and double check" look in their window that featured men's jeans and chinos. Here, too, the natural, raw look of the wood is enhanced by the warm, light yellow tinted light.

In a more "tailored" mood, Bergdorf gets its "act" together and creates a very neutral and very monochromatic Mondrian pattern on its neutral toned back wall. The featured merchandise consists of brown suits and coats. The wood strips and the lathe strips are organized to become "frames" behind the merchandise.

LUMBER 89

BERGDORF GOODMAN, Fifth Ave., New York, NY
VP of Visual Presentation: Linda Fargo
Window Visual Dir.: David Hoey

MACY'S, Herald Square, New York, NY
VP of VM: Mark Minichiello
Window Dir.: Sam Joseph
Sr. Exec. Windows: Gil Croy

ZEGNA, Fifth Ave., New York, NY
Corp. V.M. Director: Tim Knorr

MAN'S WORLD

T. EATON, Toronto, ON, Canada
Div. Mgr. of V.M. Presentation: Eric Woodward
Mgr.: Sonia Hamori
Photographer: Guntar Kravis

MARSHALL FIELD, State St., Chicago, IL
V.M. Director: Amy Meadows
Designer: D. Milano

Setting the scene for men's apparel. Whether it is dress-up, dress-down Friday, business clothing, or just hanging around casual wear the display setting sets the theme and the look. What the well dressed businessman will wear is laid out for him in his suite high over the city he has conquered. The plush leather chair, the rich mahogany wood panels and the photo blow up stretched across the apartment "window" serve as foils for the outfit on the draper. The shoes sit on the floor and the coat is casually draped over the arm of the chair. The "red apple" on the table is the hero's reward.

T. Eaton's Father's Day theme— Thanks Dad— was played out in a series of room settings with masculine appeal while Marshall Field moved the action over to the local bar where the guys get together. The suit forms are set up on the bar stools which front the pseudo-bar. There is a feeling of "good sports" emanating from this cleverly suggested setting.

Success goes to the top and at Saks Fifth Ave. the photomural is a view from the top and it provides the setting for the dressed-for-success outfits presented on the suit forms. Stacks of the *Wall Street Journal* serve as elevations for the shoes and the must-have leather briefcase.

SAKS FIFTH AVE., New York, NY
V.P. of Visual Merchandising: Ken Smart
Window Visual Dir.: Randy Yaw

BERGDORF, Store for Men, Fifth Ave., New York, NY
Dir. of Visual Presentation, Men's Store: Harry Bader

SAKS FIFTH AVE.
New York, NY
V.P. of V.M.: Ken Smart
Dir. if Windows:
Randy Yaw

All it seems to take are some photos—black and white in color—to create noteworthy settings for display. Saks Fifth Ave.'s Man of Distinction is dressed in neutral colors and balanced by the three black and white "sports-oriented" photographs. They tier in with the message on the front glass: "Sport of Fashion."

Bergdorf's Store for Men shows off travel-right outfits with a selection of nostalgic Americana black and white photos. They are "gum cornered" onto the back wall as though they were pages in some old photo album found in some grandmother's attic. The tires in the foreground contrast with the "ice cream" colored clothes but also carry through the "on the road" theme.

The invisible man in Paul Stuart's window may seem somewhat overdressed for a game of golf but, here too, nostalgia pays off and scores points. Visible—though barely—on the rear wall is an "antique" golf poster and in the foreground is a golf cart with ties uncurling and floating out into space. The fun in the Paul Stuart signature windows is often what is not highlighted but what has to be searched for.

Cole Haan really steps out with a blow-up of the shoe revving up and taking off on a motorbike. To suggest the "hand stitching" and the "detailing" of the classic shoe, the designers used the terra cotta colored suit form (a symbol of custom tailoring) and the giant needle and thread in the foreground. A.Testoni's photo shows up the shoe in full color and the "racing man" in the subtle shadowy tones while the actual shoes and accessories are neatly arranged on the floor of the window.

PAUL STUART,
Madison Ave., New York, NY
Creative Director: Thomas Beebe
Co-Visual Directors: Jerry
Freedella & Michael Verbert
Design Team: Thomas Dang VU

COLE HAAN, Fifth Ave., New York, NY
V.M. Director: Elena C. Petrocco
Visual Merchandiser: Carl Hatchett
Production/Design Consultants: MCN Design

A. TESTONI, New York, NY

BARNEYS, (ABOVE AND RIGHT) **Madison Ave.
New York, NY
Creative Director: Simon Doonan
Sr. V.P. Creative Services: David New
V.P. Creative Services: Adamo DiGregorio**

Barneys on Madison Ave. in New York City is noted for its menswear department. When Barneys first opened back in the 1920s it was solely devoted to clothing boy and man. Today the store features the lines of many top designers. Shown here are some recent approaches to the presentation of the store's menswear collections.

Brioni's archival collection takes up most of the rich, yellow-gold ambiance. With the exception of the tuxedo on the far right all the other garments are vintage Brioni designs and the little placards identify their time and place in menswear "history."

For the made-to-measure clothing the outfits were displayed on "old" suit forms with cast iron bases. The walls are covered with leather hides of assorted shapes. The old ironing board, hung on the far left, recalls the old-fashioned, hand tailoring process used in making suits to order.

The Oxford Clothing are somewhere to be found in the clutter of props and the collage of antique signs, photos, and graphics on the rear wall. This is not a window one quickly passes by. It demands that the shopper stop and study the wealth

of details collected therein. The props included leather bound volumes, an aged oil painting, spools of yarn used in textile weaving, vintage leather luggage, gilt frames—and so much more.

Cascading golf umbrellas add pizzazz to the window that features a line-up of five outfits on "antique" suit forms. Leather belts are shown draped over the folded trousers, shoes are raised up on thin metal stems and a leather bag rests on the floor.

MAN'S WORLD

BARNEYS, (ABOVE AND BELOW) **Madison Ave., New York, NY**
Creative Director: Simon Doonan
Sr. V.P. Creative Services: David New
V.P. Creative Services: Adamo DiGregorio

MOSCHINO, Madison Ave., New York, NY
Display Director: David Griffin

If once is good, twice could be better! Mirror images are instant replays viewed from a different position, location, or even point of view.

Moschino presents a modern day version of Alice through the looking glass—or, at least, a surreal view of it. Figures seem to be disappearing into or reappearing from the oval mirrors that line two walls of the display space. A hand, a leg, an entire body is being swallowed up or being spewed out. It all adds up to mirror magic!

Escada stretches its tiny window space on E. 57th St. by the use of mirrors and illusions created by the mirrored panels. In one display the mylar or mirror panel is partially overlaid with strips of colored acetate so that the back of the blue dress is seen in a variety of colors in the mirrored reflection. In the other display, the mannequin is backed up by a serpentine panel of yellow plastic and can be seen broken up into many small parts in the multi-framed, mirrored door to the side. It is all an illusion.

The tri-fold mirror in the Tiffany window shows viewers approaching the shadow box from any direction the soaped-up face of the man and his Tiffany jewelry. Clever!!

MIRROR IMAGES 97

ESCADA: (ABOVE AND ABOVE RIGHT) E. 57th St., New York, NY
Director of Visual Merchandising: Anthony Battaglia

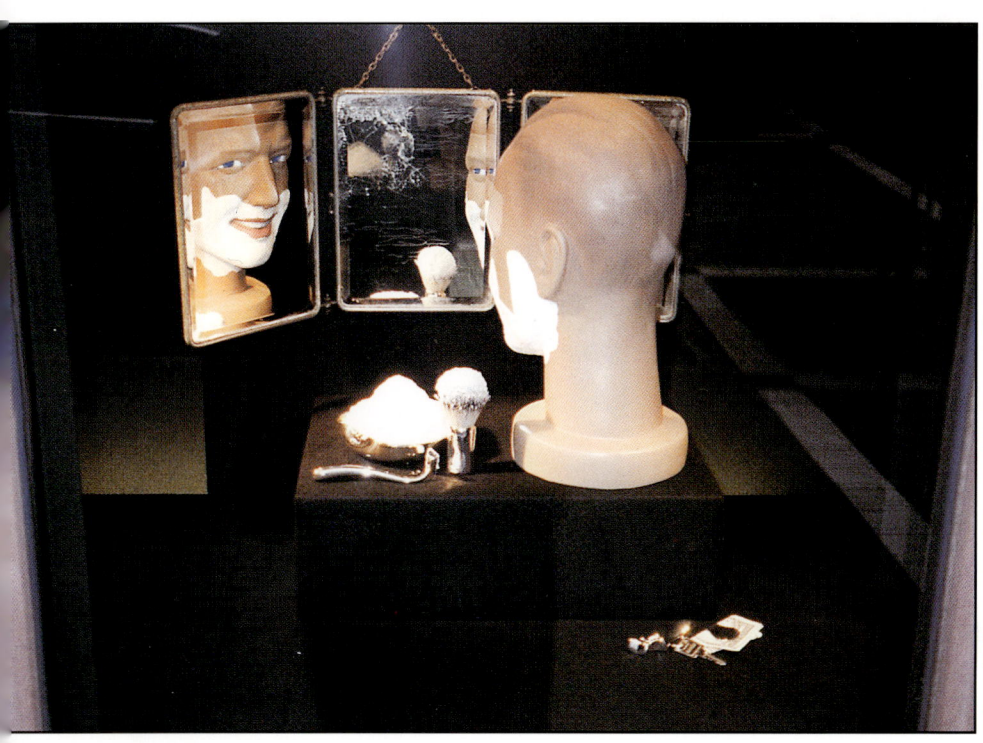

TIFFANY, Munich, Germany
Peter Rank, Deko Rank

BIRKS, Montreal, QC Canada
Display Designer/Consultant:
Lucy-Ann Bouwman
Photography: Massimo

MOTHER'S DAY

BIRKS, (ALL) Montreal, QC Canada
Display Designer/Consultant:
Lucy-Ann Bouwman
Photography: Massimo

Birks of Montreal, an upscale and highly respected jewelry/gift store with over a century of service to the community, turned back the clock to celebrate Mother's Day. The display designer/consultant, Lucy-Ann Bouwman, took her inspiration from the American first grade reader of half a century ago—"Off to School"—and in a series of windows not only showed Dick, Sally, Jane, Mother and Father in period style illustrations but also manufactured "images" of those days gone by.

To feature elegant silver apples and fruit, a traditional apple-corer from even earlier in the century shares the display space with the illustration and the red checkered background pattern that unifies the series of windows. When one thinks of mother and "comfort foods" what could be more traditional than Campbell's Chicken Noodle Soup in the familiar red and white cans? The cans are lined up vertically to provide an arresting back-up for the silver soup ladle floating up front. New at the end of the 1990's is the concept of the "working mother"—away from home. Gifts for her were cleverly displayed along with a blouse made and trimmed with tea towel fabric and some dish towels—all suspended from inverted, cut-in-half, wooden hangers.

Whatever the ideal gift may be, it can be found gift wrapped and be-ribboned in the miniature market wagon set in front of the "reader" illustration of the entire family off on a family adventure.

T. EATON & CO., (ABOVE AND RIGHT) Toronto, ON Canada
Div. Manager of V.M. Presentation: Eric Woodward
Manager: Sonia Hamori
Photography: Guntar Kravis

Simply stated but repeated often enough to be emphatic. That is how Eaton's Toronto store celebrated Mother's Day with a store-wide promotion.

Building on a concept that was developed for the Spring/Easter trim, the display designers used semi-sheer, silk-screened hanging banners throughout the store featuring the pink tulip and the message—"Thanks Mom." In the window, the white abstract mannequins in their summery pastel pink and white separates were shown in a warm, blushing pink ambiance. The message appears on the rear wall which is blocked off with squares of assorted pink tones.

Inside the store, in the many departments where gifts for mother can be purchased, the silk-screened banners were combined with silk tulips in vases and the tulip patterned paper that was used by the Eaton display team for the spring trim. The hat boxes that formerly were used as display props in the dress department now serve as elevations in the lingerie department. Note the fun, tulip paper veneered headboard in the linens area.

T. EATON & CO., (RIGHT AND BELOW)
Toronto, ON Canada
Div. Manager of V.M. Presentation: Eric Woodward
Manager: Sonia Hamori
Photography: Guntar Kravis

SAKS FIFTH AVE., New York, NY
VP of V.M.: Ken Smart
Window Director: Randy Yaw

If there is theater, there must be music. Music is a universal thing and can blend with or enhance any product presentation. Whether it means taking the copy line from a song title or showing the music score or just bringing out the instruments for a bow, music is a universal theme. It can be real instruments borrowed from a school marching band or from a music supply store in exchange for a credit card in the window or it can be imagined instruments made of wire, wood, cut out of foamcore, twigs and branches or even photo blow-ups.

At Saks it may be a bit Braque—or maybe Picasso—but the cubistic image of the oddly shaped stringed instrument in red picks up and reinforces the red embroidery of the sweater. The earthy patches of the color, in the background, add to the feeling of the cubist painting of the early 20th century.

The song lingers on in Bergdorf's windows where the mannequin, formally gowned in white, opens up a surreal white cabinet in the all white surroundings to reveal stacked cellos and violas. The richly colored woods contrast with all that white. In a blast of brass—or is it pure gold—the shimmering metallic gown is complemented by the big brass instruments tied up and suspended off of gold silk ropes.

BERGDORF GOODMAN, (ABOVE AND LEFT) Fifth Ave., New York, NY
VP of Visual Presentation: Linda Fargo
Window Director: David Hoey

HENRI BENDEL, Fifth Ave., New York, NY
Dir. of Visual Presentation: Barbara Putnam

Sizzle and Pizzazz! Glimmer sand glow and haloes of light! Neon can be glitz or it can be glamour. Shown here are some clever uses of neon in window displays.

Henri Bendel's display of hot pink merchandise becomes griddle hot and sizzles between the red of the background wall and floor and the brilliant cerise/lake colored light strips that are jack-strawed throughout the open backed window. The dangle and swirl of the black electric cords add greater kinetic energy to this hot! hot! hot! look. They also add to the impromptu attitude of the setting.

Bally's GIANT background photo blow-up gets additional impact from the brilliant line of light that adds to the strong vertical statement. The neon also forms a rectangular frame on the floor to accentuate the actual outfit now dwarfed by the super, super, two story high background photo.

It's the glow that matters in the Marshall Field display where the neon outlines the two pedestals that rise up from the angled sheet of frosted plexiglass. Counteracting the sharp neon haloes are the soft patches of colored light on the rear wall that seem to blend and blur.

Ferregamo makes a single neon frame go far when it is placed against a mirror that replays the cutting blue light pattern over and over again. The mirror and the neon outline add depth to the simple presentation.

Prado makes the most out of its minimal display by placing it in a neon cage. If it weren't for the illuminated, dimensional form, the hanging merchandise would almost disappear from view.

BALLY, Fifth Ave., New York, NY

FERREGAMO, Fifth Ave., New York, NY
Director of Visuals: John Krenek
Asst. Director: Jesse Barber

MARSHALL FIELD, State St., Chicago, IL
V.M. Director: Jamie Becker, Dir. of Visual Marketing, Dayton Hudson
V.M. Director, State St.: Amy Meadows
Window Director: Donna Milano-Johnson

PRADA, Fifth Ave., New York, NY

BERGDORF GOODMAN, (ABOVE AND RIGHT) **Fifth Ave., New York, NY**
VP of Visual Presentation: Linda Fargo
Window Director: David Hoey

And the SHOW goes on! Display is Theater and Theater is always exciting and a show-y way to bring attention to the merchandise being presented.

Bergdorf Goodman tied in with the theater concept and thus takes us on stage—and back stage. From backstage we see the backs of the theatrical flats, the props, the bare and exposed lighting, the ropes. It is all spectacle and glamour as we get this usually unseen view of the play. On stage, the fashionably dressed mannequins appear to be co-starring in a fantasy version of a Midsummer Night's Dream (the movie had just been released) and we become the spectators out front as the magic is fully revealed.

Another revelation took place at Marshall Field's when they took center stage with their "Sugar" promotion. With simple, almost cartoony and over the top sketchy drawings of rooms, draperies and prosceniums, the designers created arresting flat settings for the realistic mannequins. On the front glass, the copy explains "the action and the setting."

ON STAGE 107

MARSHALL FIELD'S, (ABOVE AND BELOW) **State St., Chicago, IL**
Window Director: Amy Meadows

ST JOHN BOUTIQUE, Fifth Ave., New York, NY
Creative Director: Kelly Gray

A favorite attention-getting device in window display is to play with scale or the proportion of things in the viewing area. When a prop or background makes the mannequin or form seem to shrink to miniature size or loom up as a giant amid Lilliputians, the shopper on the street is usually intrigued and interested enough to come up closer to the window and check things out.

On the following pages are some BIG—really BIG—props that make the mannequins and forms seem almost like well dressed and coiffed Barbie dolls. At St. John Boutique it is the giant shoe behind the mannequin in the classic red suit that does it while at Printemps it is the supersized handbag. Great, great fun is the oversized bowl of pasta and clams and the fork that is drawing up the Moschino gown from the mixture of dimensional and drawn food. Another great touch in the Moschino window is the use of truly heroic sized red and white checkered cloth—a real Italian cliché! Overdone? Sure! But who cares. It works!

OVERSCALED 109

MOSCHINO, Madison Ave., New York, NY
Designer: David Griffin

PRINTEMPS, Paris, France

BARNEYS, (ABOVE AND RIGHT)
Madison Ave., New York, NY
Creative Director: Simon Doonan
Sr. VP of Creative Services:
David New
VP of Creative Services:
Adamo DiGregorio

The mammoth owl that overfills the back of Barneys window is wonderfully conceived and executed in corrugated board. Note the size of the scissors in the foreground, in scale with the owl. In another flight of scale Barneys dreams up and dresses a humungous scarecrow of a cut out in a black dress to emphasize the collection of black dresses paraded on the mere mortal sized headless but stretch necked mannequins.

BERGDORF GOODMAN, Fifth Ave., New York, NY
VP of Visual Presentation: Linda Fargo
Window Visual Director: David Hoey

Nobody really needs reading glasses to read the letters blown up to serve as backgrounds for the black and white clad mannequin in Bergdorf's window. Even the push pins—also black—are way oversized.

It would take a "jolly green giant" top wear this fantasy mask created out of gold plated wash basins and trimmed with assorted gilt faucets and hardware. The red mask in Sherle Wagner's window is finished with superscaled ruffles of gold lame fabric for a total attention-getter.

SHERLE WAGNER
E. 57th St., New York, NY
Designer: Anne Kong

GUCCI, Fifth Ave., New York, NY
Corp. Dir. of Visual Presentation:
James Knight

What would display people do without photography? In recent years—with ever tightening and often disappearing budgets—display persons have come to rely on two dimensional graphs and photo blow ups to create the time and place in their display settings. With chainstore display set-ups like The Gap, J.Crew and Banana Republic, the oversized, over-scaled drama of a photo blow up in an open back window has helped to unify the chain's look across the country. Throughout this edition the reader will be aware of how often photography is used. On the next few pages we will show some unusual approaches to how to use photographs.

Repetition does it at Gucci. The pattern created by the frames of the same black and white image serves as a formal and symmetrical background for the black suit. The repetition of the image of the same outfit, in the photo, shows just how important the look is.

Barneys fills—figuratively and literally—the window with color photographs. They surround, inundate and almost overwhelm the line-up of garments on the abstract figures. Somewhere there is a message in there!

BARNEYS, Madison Ave.
New York, NY
Creative Director: Simon Doonan
Sr. V.P. Creative Services: David New
V.P.. Creative Services:
Adamo DiGregorio

BERGDORF GOODMAN, (ABOVE AND RIGHT) Fifth Ave., New York, NY
Dir. of Visual Presentation: Linda Fargo

The novelty in Bergdorf's window is the ballgown made of black and white photos and pages of fashion magazines. Saluting David Bailey and "The Birth of The Cool," the bright yellow swath of seamless paper sets off and emphasizes the mannequin in the paper gown. The rest of the backwall and floor is papered with more black and white photos. The other mannequins are dressed in black and photography equipment underscores the importance of the photos.

Taking advantage of their tall windows, Bergdorf Goodman's display goes way, way up with framed black and white photos. Black painted opera chairs are piled up on the floor and the spindly construction becomes a series of elevations for the gray, stylized mannequins.

LORD & TAYLOR, Fifth Ave., New York, NY
Window Director, N.Y.: Jan Topercer
Creative Director: Manoel Renha

Bigger is better—when blowing up photographs to serve as backgrounds. Shown here are a variety of "scenes" and "settings" that rely upon the photograph behind to make the merchandise up front believable.

Zegna goes "casual" and the casual setting is a giant blow-up of a country scene. Lord & Taylor sets a seaside mood with a long horizontal image of a pier leading out to where the sea and the sky meet.

To emphasize the "big city, bright lights" pattern on the gowns, Moschino turns the window into a luxurious apartment with a fabulous view of the illuminated city. The white window mullions serve to divide the setting: up front on the black and white tiled floor is the living room and behind the "window" is the terrace with the panoramic view. The depth perception is fabulous—as is the overall effect.

A somewhat more peaceful view: a bridge over calm waters. Chanel uses this as a background for the lavender and gray outfit. The black and white photo mural complements the gray tones. Note the silver gray mannequin stands on a bridge of her own.

ZEGNA, Fifth Ave., New York, NY
Corp. V.M. Dir.: Tim Knorr

PHOTOGRAPHY 115

MOSCHINO, Madison Ave., New York, NY
Display: David Griffin

CHANEL, E. 57th St., New York, NY
Display: Todd Schearer

When you blow up a photo and use it as a setting it can be very effective but here are some really different approaches to making the photo come off the wall and become part of the action.

Valentino has it all together. The photo blow up has been cut into pieces of a jigsaw puzzle and then reassembled to make the point. There are enough extra pieces left to show that it is a jig saw puzzle and also to add some excitement to the space.

If you can't get in to see Prada's runway fashion show— Prada will bring it out to you in the window. Life size photos of the runway models are mounted and cut out and they come "alive" as they strut out in the window space. A simple paper panel shuts off part of the pale green store beyond and puts the viewer on the street into the best "seat" in the house.

Bergdorf chops up a large blow up and then hangs the odd shaped slivers just enough off kilter to get the desired reaction from the shopper in the street. Now the viewer has to stop and sort of refocus on what is going on behind the blond mannequins in pink and gray.

VALENTINO, Fifth Ave., New York, NY
Display: Jordi Lopez

**PRADA, Madison Ave.
New York, NY**

BERGDORF GOODMAN, Fifth Ave., New York, NY
Dir. of Visual Presentation: Linda Fargo

BERGDORF FOR MEN, Fifth Ave., New York, NY
Visual Director Mens: Harry Bader

Get out your easels, your canvases, paint brushes and palettes—your finished artwork for a "Picture This" display. If you don't have the props, they are readily available in the art supply houses, in print shops and in galleries—often just for the borrowing in exchange for a credit card in the window.

Bergdorf for Men paints a great picture of blue and white with a bright blue floor, a blue paint spattered drop cloth, paint cans dripping blue paint, brushes and rollers, frames and stretched canvases. The blue Nike cast plus the blue canvases highlight the color story.

Saks is seeing gold in fashion and the gold on gold "paintings" and the ombred gold background along with the glittering gold gown—all washed in yellow light—make this a "gilt edged" picture to behold.

Barneys goes all out with paintings and artwork galore. The store is saluting the retrospective acrylic art of Stephen Caliguiri. In sharp contrast to the brilliant palette of the paintings are the black and white fashions shown on the white abstract mannequins.

Arrange your own "retrospective" or "salute" by contacting local artists or galleries who will be delighted for such exposure.

SAKS FIFTH AVE., New York, NY
V.P. of V.M.: Ken Smart
Window Director: Randy Yaw

BARNEYS, (ABOVE AND BELOW) **Madison Ave., New York, NY**
Creative Director: Simon Doonan
Sr. V.P. Creative Services: David New
V.P. Creative Services: Adamo Di Gregorio

The displays shown here all appeared in the Saks Fifth Ave. windows. The "artwork" included anything from "thumbprint" smears and daubs on the front glass and rear wall with the dressed headless mannequin caught in between, to bold slashes of brilliant colors on canvas to accentuate the chartreuse and red violet evening fashions on the white abstract mannequins. A "monochromatic" painting in red serves as a background for dimensional black forms either attached to or free standing in front of the art with a stylized mannequin, accent lighted, in black and white.

It's easier to Picture This—when the artwork actually refers to the fashions being presented as they do with the three dress forms—two in prints—that serves as inspiration for the large painted panel behind the central form.

SAKS FIFTH AVE., (above and right) New York, NY
V.P. of V.M.: Ken Smart
Windows Visuals Director: Randy Yaw

SAKS FIFTH AVE., (above and right)
New York, NY
V.P. of V.M.: Ken Smart
Windows Visuals Director: Randy Yaw

Simple solutions

T. EATON & CO., Toronto, ON Canada
Div. Manager of V.M. Presentation: Eric Woodward
Manager: Sonia Hamori
Photography: Guntar Kravis

A "simple solution" usually calls for a simple, straightforward display. Eaton's statement is a warm, off-white wall and a variety of separates and accessories pinned up on it. The garments are on hangers that hook on to hooks "cemented" onto the wall while the hat and shoes are defying gravity and pinned up.

Carson Pirie Scott rips back the shrouded curtain to reveal the Polo Jeans Co. "Shades of White" collection. On what looks like a giant drop cloth of white muslin, a helter skelter arrangement of pin ups shows the assorted separates and accessories that make up the collection. Note how often the designer's name and logo is "casually" reintroduced into the mix to make a brand name impact.

CARSON PIRIE SCOTT,
State St., Chicago, IL
V.P. Visual Merchandising:
Rick Schlenther
Regional V.M. Director: Ted Georgiou
Display Director State Street:
Bruce Booker

LORD & TAYLOR, Fifth Ave., New York, NY
V.P. of V.M.: Cal Partridge
V.M. Director Fifth Ave.: Jan Topercer
Creative Director: Manoel Renha

More like stretched taut and tied up are the separates in Lord & Taylor's window. The dress form in the center wears a complete outfit and two others re-shown—one to either side—against the red stained wood panels in the emphatic vertical frames. Wire, clips and toggle bolts all combine to create this unusual merchandise "pin up."

Barneys pins up a single jacket on a hanger and complements it with a lay-down of jackets, ties and shoes below the rough plywood panel. Note how the details of the tailoring are pointed out on the panel that carries the single Kilgour, French & Stanbury jacket.

Wanthe and Ferregamo both use clothes hooks to casually pin up the jackets in their displays. While horse pictures, bridles, harnesses and even a saddle provide the "horsy" attitude for Wathne sports jackets, Ferregamo's outfit is sort of layered on the hook on the "stone" background with an array of ties draped over the chair back and a pair of shoes is set on the floor.

**BARNEYS, Madison Ave.,
New York, NY
Creative Director: Simon Doonan
Sr. V.P. Creative Services:
David New
V.P. Creative Services:
Adamo Di Gregorio**

**FERREGAMO, Fifth Ave., New York, NY
Director of Visuals: John Krenek**

**WATHNE, W. 57th St., New York, NY
Display Director: Jim Amen**

LORD & TAYLOR, Fifth Ave., New York, NY

ZCMI, Salt Lake City, UT
Visuals Director: Mike Stephens
Designers: Diane Call & Celeste Cecchini

Pink is pretty, but pink can be passionate. Pink is pastel but it can be vivid, vital and utterly vivacious. On view here are some of the different attitudes of pink and how they were portrayed.

Lord & Taylor is "In The Pink" with pale pink gowns shown against a vivid pink background. Pink posies are polka-dotted over all.

ZCMI presented a wholesome pink suit amid bare branches abloom with rich, ripe tissue magnolia blossoms. The chromed screen has some squares filled with pink tissue while more of the tissue-fabricated flowers are scattered on the floor. In a more dramatic mood, ZCMI presents a vibrant pink "Conversation Piece" against gold leafed panels floating behind and a casual arrangement of metallic pink chairs.

Pulling out all the stops for a truly passionate pink is Saks Fifth Ave.'s window which is hot with red light and that color surrounds the semi-abstract mannequin in a pink on pink flower splattered gown. A loose floral sketch, in gold leaf on a lucite panel, hangs between the mannequin and the florid rear wall.

ZCMI, Salt Lake City, UT
Visuals Director: Mike Stephens
Designers: Diane Call & Celeste Cecchini

SAKS FIFTH AVE, New York, NY
VP of V. M.: Ken Smart
Window Director: Randy Yaw

Surrounded by snow and ice, by gray skies and gloomier vistas, by tossed aside Christmas trees and brittle, bare branches, is it any wonder that one's mind and soul wanders off to warmer climes, blue skies and ever lush, green foliage? It is time to escape! It is Resort/Cruise time and a time to unveil clothes and accessories designed for the tropics.

Marshall Field's Marketplace promotion took on a tropical setting with the bamboo and raffia/straw matting vendor's cart surrounded by straw baskets of assorted shapes and sizes. The abstract mannequin is scantily clad with a mini-raffia edged sarong that ties her back into the setting.

MARSHALL FIELD'S, State St., Chicago, IL
Display Director: Amy Meadows
Designer: Steve Huzenga

RESORT 129

HENRI BENDEL, Fifth Ave., New York, NY
Dir. Of Visual Presentation: Graham Belman

LORD & TAYLOR, Fifth Ave., New York, NY
VP of V. M.: Cal Partridge
Creative Director: Manoel Renha

Bendel's soaring, two story high, open-back window is the perfect place for the tall palm tree and the attendant rich green foliage. A pseudo-native drum becomes a thematic riser and display "table" for the "Glamazon" product display. Jungle flowers grow up from the thick, verdant carpet. The mannequin, in pink, turns her back on the public outside but still allows a clean view of the bare-backed dress.

Bamboo, woven matting, some coconuts in their thick, dark shells and some sprouting sprays of greenery are the props in the Lord & Taylor window used to showcase the "native-inspired" outfit topped off with a straw "coolie" hat. The dark, rich lighting adds an exotic quality to the scene.

BARNEYS, Madison Ave., New York, NY
Creative Director: Simon Doonan
Sr. VP of Creative Services: David New
VP of Creative Services: Adamo Di Gregorio

Say "SALE" with style—with color—with panache. Say it like you mean it and not like something you are embarrassed to admit. Make it a celebration—make it fun—make it an event.

Never one to understate—Barneys makes a big splash with a "Clearance Sale" announcement that stretches across the whole window. In addition toi the bold statement, the display staff adds a European touch with the red bordered slashed price cards that are unashamedly pinned on to some of the garments. The shoppers can't help but get the message.

More discrete and refined is the Cole Haan sales approach. The message is sent twice; once in a yellow bordered panel at eye level and then again with cut out letters on a level with the floor displayed shoes and bags.

COLE HAAN, Fifth Ave. New York, NY
VM Director: Elena C. Petrocco
VM: Carl Hatchett

VERSACE, Fifth Ave., New York, NY

Daffys is all but shouting it from the rooftops. The in-your-face red, white and blue graphic panels jump off the back wall to announce the event.

Versace's window features a single garment on a black dress form and a vivid, hot pink panel with the SALE repeated on it several times in white. The fabric panel is set behind a black lacquered frame with thin metal rods that create the fine vertical lines over the pink panel.

DAFFYS, Fifth Ave., New York, NY
Visuals Director: Mary Costantini

PILAR ROSSI, (LEFT AND BELOW) Madison Ave., New York, NY
Designer: Marc Manigault

Pilar Rossi is an elegant designer shop that sells elegant fashions on Madison Avenue. When a SALE is planned—it takes on more elegance and refinement. Shown here are two truly handsome SALE windows that neither demean the bargain hunting shopper or the merchandise and the designer. Class shows!

SALE 133

H&M, Amsterdam

PRINTEMPS, Paris

C&A, Amsterdam

BARNEYS, (TOP AND ABOVE) Madison Ave., New York, NY
Creative Director: Simon Doonan
Sr. VP of Creative Services David New
VP of Creative Services: Adamo DiGregerio

Repetition can be boring—or it can be a reinforcement for an idea. Sometimes seeing the same image or object repeated over and over again can make an indelible impression but just repeating—like hiccuping or stuttering—can be painful or even annoying. A good displayperson finds new and surprising ways of making the statement over and over and still leave us wanting to see it again and again. Barneys assumes that we will get it right because we are offered seven forms in a row—all positioned and draped in the same manner—with shoes lined up like soldiers at Parade Rest. The back wall is covered with row upon row of the same graphic repeated on and on. The variety is in the different outfits shown in the line-up.

In another display, the repetition is in the placement of the turned pedestals and the shoes on top. Also repeated ad infinitum are the sketches of the shoe on the back wall. Here, however, the repetition is broken by the casual arrangement of the figures and forms—and the feathered boa that stretches across the display.

SAY IT AGAIN 135

BARNEYS, (ALL) Madison Ave., New York, NY
Creative Director: Simon Doonan
Sr. VP of Creative Services David New
VP of Creative Services: Adamo DiGregerio

Whether using Barbie dolls or plastic Afro combs—the repetition of endless rows or squares makes for attention getting. It is the "change of pace"—or the break in the repetitive pattern like a different doll or an odd shoe—that makes these displays unique. It is the unexpected that makes them connect.

BLOOMINGDALE'S, (ABOVE AND RIGHT)
Lexington Ave., New York, NY
VP of V.M.: Jack Hruska
Creative Director: Mike Fisher
Window Manager: Harry Medina

Bloomingdale's plays the "play it again" game with bottles and cans of juice to make a punchy point in their Juicy Couture display. Note the even spacing of the cans up against the window and the scattering of the bottles on the floor beyond. An unusual "dip in the blue" is offered the swim-suited duo in Bloomingdale's swimwear window. The pair stand on myriad beakers filled with marine blue water in an all-white setting. Who says you can't walk on water?

Bergdorf believes in more is better in these windows. Hundreds of wire hangers are tangled and dangled into an amorphous setting for the abstract mannequin in the red gown. Yellow sipping straws create an abstract "dune" setting for the casually clad figures. Imagine what you could do with dozens of yellow pencils for a back-to-school promotion. All it takes is time—and imagination.

Coffee beans or dark and light chocolate wafers—whatever—they are used to fill three glass vases to point up a brown and beige color statement. In the Loro Piana display it is the light touch—on top of the innermost vase—that breaks the monotony and creates the interest.

SAY IT AGAIN & AGAIN 137

BERGDORF GOODMAN, Fifth Ave., New York, NY
VP of V.M.: Linda Fargo
Window Director: David Hoey

LORO PIANO, Madison Ave., New York, NY

BERGDORF GOODMAN, Fifth Ave., New York, NY
VP of V.M.: Linda Fargo
Window Director: David Hoey

**MOSCHINO, Madison Ave.,
New York, NY
Execution: David Griffin**

**HENRI BENDEL, Fifth Ave., New York, NY
Dir. of Visual Presentation: Graham Belman**

Moschino is dipping its colorful jeweled halter tops into the "Cool Aid" flavored glasses lined up in tiers—like technicolor wedding cakes. The pitchers are pouring out the garments and the color saturated glasses below make this a real "stopper."

Bendel parades a selection of colorful Custo designed tops in their window. Unifying the vast variety of shapers, colors, and patterns are the simple, flat cut-out forms that "wear" them. The forms are arranged in orderly rows—one atop the other—and they stretch across the brilliant red background.

SAY IT AGAIN & AGAIN & AGAIN   139

If it is cool enough to wear fur—it is rather "cool" to surround and entrap the abstract in a grid with dozens of grinning gnomes. The gnomes, the grid and the mannequin are all painted aqua to accentuate the henna colored fur at Frohlich.

Two examples of repetition played out in Tiffany windows in Munich: coils of golden rope and plastic soda bottles are the materials. In each instance it is the break from the repetition that makes the points and illustrates the merchandise being presented.

FROHLICH FURS, Munich, Germany
Design & Execution: Peter Rank, Deko Rank

TIFFANY, (ABOVE AND ABOVE LEFT) **Munich, Germany**
Design & Execution: Peter Rank, Deko Rank

140　STORE WINDOWS　No. 12

BIRKS JEWELRY, Montreal, QC, Canada
Designer: Lucy Ann Bouwman
Photographer: Massimo

In the allotted shadow box windows of the Birks Jewelry store, the display designer made some big statements using ordinary and often tossed away objects.

An old fashioned sewing machine head might have been good enough for some but not for Lucy Ann Bouwman, the designer, who had to dress her's in a custom denim outfit. Spools of thread surround the head and assorted chain stitches are tried out in different colored threads on the back fabric panel. What is featured so cleverly is the gold chain bracelet that is being "created" on the machine.

In keeping with the sewing theme, Ms. Bouwman creates a subtly shaded background out of cones of thread and ruching trim. Here again, the pattern of the lacy trimming and binding enhances the lacy quality of the gold and diamond necklace up front.

For a more "masculine" appeal—to show off watches for him—hundreds of pins are being retrieved and create magnetic magic in the small space.

BIRKS JEWELRY, (ABOVE AND RIGHT)
Montreal, QC, Canada
Designer: Lucy Ann Bouwman
Photographer: Massimo

MOSCHINO, Madison Ave., New York, NY
Design: David Griffin

Sew What? Sewing means the fine art of tailoring—of basting—binding—fitting and finishing!

Moschino creates an amusing window with multiple sewing machine heads of assorted types and vintages displayed on simple white tables of varying heights. Coming off the machines are some of Moschino's newest creations. The all-white setting serves as an effective background for the different colored garments.

Barneys goes to the spools of yarn of myriad colors to recreate the fabulous color palette of the colorful, patterned Missoni sweaters on the egghead topped dress forms. Rolls of Missoni fabrics are suspended horizontally throughout the window and the background is a montage of photos, swatches and samples of Missoni's art.

BARNEYS, Madison Ave., New York, NY
Creative Director: Simon Doonan
Sr. VP of Creative Services: David New
VP of Creative Services: Adamo DiGregorio

LORO PIANO, Madison Ave., New York, NY

Loro Piano and Saks Fifth Ave. both show off the "before and after" of fine tailoring. A basted, partially constructed jacket is shown alongside the exquisitely detailed and finished end product. Saks goes a bit further by adding some amusing props and decorative cliches to its basted version.

SAKS FIFTH AVE., New York, NY
VP of VM: Ken Smart
Window Visual Director: Randy Yaw

HENRI BENDEL, Fifth Ave., New York, NY
Director of Visuals: Barbara Putnam

Soft, silky, drapable fabrics—hung straight, swagged, stretched or swirled through a display—can sell a fabric or a color. Henri Bendel creates a rich, exotic and Asian inspired setting in the open back window which is draped over with semi-transparent panels of red, pink and royal blue. The gold embellished gowns are opulent and the keyhole arch sketched in black on the front glass along with the suspended lanterns all contribute to this Arabian Nights setting.

Panels of fabric are gently pulled and secured to create the unusual setting for the stylized mannequins in the Saks window. Bloomingdale's hangs the sheer fabric panels loosely between the upright frames to serve as a soft setting for the pastel pink and green outfits. The effective lighting on the rear wall not only complements the fashions up front but helps to emphasize the soft texture of the background panels.

Sheer fabrics of assorted lengths are dropped and draped throughout the Barneys display window to enhance the presentation of the straightforward Commes Des Garcons merchandise. Note how the fabrics are hung and looped overhead to make individual display areas for each dressed abstract mannequin. The sheer fabrics combine orange and blue panels for added interest.

SHEER MADNESS 145

BARNEYS, Madison Ave., New York, NY
Creative Director: Simon Doonan
Sr. V.P. Creative Services: David New
V.P. Creative Services: Adamo Di Gregorio

SAKS FIFTH AVE., New York, NY
V.P. of V.M. Ken Smart
Window Visual Director: Randy Yaw

BLOOMINGDALE'S, Lexington Ave., New York, NY
V.P. of V.M.: Jack Hruska
Creative Director: Mike Fisher
Window Manager: Harry Medina

LORD & TAYLOR, Fifth Ave., New York, NY
VP Visual Merchandising: Cal Paqrtridge
Creative Director: Manoel Renha

MARSHALL FIELD, State St., Chicago, IL
VP of Visual Merchandising for Dayton-Hudson: Jamie Becker
Window Director, State St.: Amy Meadows
Photographer: Susan Kezon

Lord & Taylor takes aim and really is on target with its fashion presentation backed up by the giant bull's eye target. Quivers are stuck into the white gravel covered floor and spots of colored light pick out the feathered ends of the arrows.

Marshall Field isn't fooling when it takes aim. They are showing knives—and throwing them to make a point. Some of the Wusthop Trident knives have already scored high as they stick out of the black spaces in the high score zone of the target.

SPORTING LIFE

SONY STYLE, (ALL)
Madison Ave., New York, NY
VP Retail: Helen Bratcher
Visual Events Director: Christine Belish

Sony surfs the Net with these amusing, clever and decidedly shopper stopping windows in which the Sony products—mostly small in size—gain in prominence from the propping. The sail surf board floats across cut-out waves in one of the tall and narrow windows and the sail is polka dotted with CDs. A bendable figure floats in a rubber tube with his laptop. "Street Savvy" combines fashion with sports with Sony products such as boom-boxes, radios and miniature TVs. "Hang 10 KB" has a bendable form, dressed for work, riding in on a giant "mouse" over the waves while assorted laptops and computers bob up and down between the waves.

BIRKS of MONTREAL, Montreal, QC, Canada
Lucy Ann Bouwman
Photography: Massimo

Birks of Canada under the creative direction of Lucy Ann Bouwman takes on winter sports in a series of shadow box windows. The Tiffany style windows feature a rear wall that can be illuminated from below and the precious merchandise is always added—almost as an afterthought.

With snow and ice being the usual in Montreal and so much a part of the outdoor lifestyle, Ms. Bouwman takes items such as ice skates, toboggans and hockey pucks to build her displays around. A nice touch is the puck breaking through the glass with the featured watched attached to the hockey stick. The cool blue light on the rear walls sets the wintry theme.

BIRKS of MONTREAL, (ABOVE AND LEFT)
Montreal, QC, Canada
Lucy Ann Bouwman
Photography: Massimo

BLOOMINGDALES, Lexington Ave., New York, NY
VP of Visual Merchandising: Jack Hruska
Creative Director: Mike Fisher
Window Manager: Harry Medina

Summertime and the living is easy-relaxed-casual and fun! Bloomingdales sees summertime as the time for state fairs, carnivals and riding the carousel. The window is filled with wonderful, polychromed, cavorting "wood" animals that we remember from our childhood—or remember seeing in old photographs. As for the carousel itself, the gaudy merry-go-round is suggested by the ornate rococo framed mirrors on the rear wall which is painted with colored light. The sawdust and confetti strewn floor carries through the carny imagery.

Saks Fifth Avenue takes its cue from the blow up of the New Yorker magazine cover that brims over with drawings of places to go and things to do in the summer in New York. In keeping with the cartoonish quality of the cover, cartoony, cut-out foamcore figures are dressed in the colorful, casual clothes just right for a day out in the Big Apple in the summertime.

Barneys adds to the heat of summer by taking their summer fashions out of doors for a barbeque. Just in case the charcoal in the grill doesn't work—the mannequins have taken along frying pans, toasters, and microwave ovens and assorted other plug-in cookware. This one is really cooking—and plugged in to the season.

Henri Bendel's summertime setting is the park where moms and daughters come out to play and show off their matching outfits. In the vignette setting, the out-of-doors is implied by the dripping wisteria foliage wreathed in the grape vining and the hanging swings. A fun and effective way to show the matching fashions.

SAKS FIFTH AVE., New York, NY
VP of Visual Merchandising: Ken Smart
Dir. of Window Visuals: Randy Yaw

HENRI BENDEL, Fifth Avenue, New York, NY
Display Director: Danuta Ryder

BARNEYS, Madison Ave., New York, NY
Creative Director: Simon Doonan
Sr. VP of Creative Services: David New
VP of Creative Services: Adamo Di Gregorio

MOSCHINO, Madison Ave., New York, NY
Display Director: David Griffin

Moschino visualizes the summertime as a roadside stand; weathered slats of wood, a striped awning, bushels, baskets and boxes brimming over with farm-fresh fruits and vegetables—and a colorful assortment of Moschino fashion accessories. This 3-D "painting" was part of a Madison Avenue salute to the arts.

At Bloomingdales, the young twosome are kicking up some sand on a beach in some romantic, faraway place as evidenced by the artwork on the back panel. She is holding the "key" to what is happening-and the fashion solution.

BLOOMINGDALES, Lexington Ave., New York, NY
VP of Visual Merchandising: Jack Hruska
Creative Director: Mike Fisher
Window Manager: Harry Medina

SUMMERTIME 153

PRADA, (ABOVE AND LEFT) **Madison Ave., New York, NY**

Prada is all set to set sail on the cool, cool blue waters with a series of sea-going, summertime vignettes. The glowing blue sky/sea background panel backs up the molded white plastic elements and the wood planked floor that turns these open backed windows into parts of an elegant yacht somewhere off the coast of Greece.

BERGDORF GOODMAN, (above and above right)
Fifth Ave., New York, NY
V.P. of V.M.: Linda Fargo
Assoc. Creative Director: David Hoey
Production Manager: Michael Metroka

Back in the 1920s and 1930s when Surrealism became an art trend and Dali made his leap through a plate glass window because somebody changed something in his fur-lined bathtub display, shoppers have been fascinated, amused, and even delighted with the enigma of surreal art and surreal display presentations.

These displays in Bergdorf Goodman's windows may defy rational explanation but they are certainly created and crafted to attract the shopper and keep her/him interested not only as they peruse the propping, but study the artfully displayed merchandise. Westward Ho! seems to be the explanation for the western inspired fashions and the pony skin print skirt. A "wagon" is loaded and stacked high for the trek to the wild, wild west and the mannequin seated on the rocker atop the piled up provisions and luggage seems to have the horizon in sight.

Kill the piano player? Why? The Rapunzel-like mannequin is about to take off via the wagon wheel light fixture leaving the display space an untidy mess. It is the clutter, the mess, the up-turned upheaval that draws the shopper and also asks her to make sense of the mayhem.

Truly surreal are the displays that combine unrelated and confusing props with the stylish merchandise. Clusters of old wire screened gym light fixtures, worn and broken wooden shutters, a chicken wire form with a scale for a heart and a dove in a glass cylinder? Upright crates with giant scissors, scraps of crumpled paper, a life-size wooden artist's mannikin, an antique doll head and some twigs and branches—all being hoisted with ropes and pulleys? It is like a dream sequence in a Hitchcock movie or a Dali done in 3-D.

BERGDORF GOODMAN, (ABOVE AND LEFT)
Fifth Ave., New York, NY
V.P. of V.M.: Linda Fargo
Assoc. Creative Director: David Hoey
Production Manager: Michael Metroka

"Off with your overcoat—off with your gloves" goes the very old song. You may not be "burning with love" but you may want to bask in the tropic sunshine while refreshing yourself in the blue, blue lagoon—or the sea. If sea and surf are not available—well, there are options!

Stuck close to home and no lake or lagoon at hand? Do what Saks and Bloomingdale's suggests. Blow up some inflatable pools and take the "plunge." At Bloomingdale's, the vertically placed inflatable tubs add an interesting pattern of soft, wavy lines behind the stylish mannequins. At Saks, dad and the kids are ready to enjoy a "backyard" swim. Green grass matting, inflatable toys, goggles and snorkeling gear help to fill out the setting.

Moschino creates a deserted island in their window which is surrounded by sea, sky and illusionary lighting. The three bikini-ed torsos are set on a sandy beach with a palm tree rising up from behind.

Saks creates a painted, theatrical flat that floats against the blue, blue background while lighting effects produce the shimmering watery waves on the floor in this menswear swim window.

SAKS FIFTH AVE., New York, NY
VP of V.M.: Ken Smart
Window Visual Dir.: Randy Yaw

BLOOMINGDALE'S, Lexington Ave., New York, NY
VP of V.M.: Jack Hruska
Creative Director: Mike Fischer

SWIMWEAR 157

MOSCHINO, Madison Ave., New York, NY
Window Director: David Griffin

SAKS FIFTH AVE., New York, NY
VP of V.M.: Ken Smart
Window Visual Dir.: Randy Yaw

DKNY, (LEFT AND BELOW) Fifth Ave., New York, NY

Fall is synonymous with the Arts; the opera, ballet and theater seasons, gallery showings, galas and grand openings. The theater is close to the hearts of many displaypersons so is it any wonder that so many turn to their " first love" for inspiration?

In the open back windows of DKNY, the display designers took us "backstage" as though the mannequins were the performers about to enter on stage. Flats, kleig lights, miles of coiled electrical wires, ropes, weights and boxes—even strip lights "up front"—all add a sense of theatrical excitement and suggest "curtain going up" on a new season or a new line. The designers mixed metaphors—including reels of film—but what's the difference—it's all Theater!!

Barneys takes us on stage with costumes, curtains, lights and lots and lots of glitter, glitz and pizzazz. Forms are bedecked with fanciful outfits, racks are filled with outfits ready to "go on" and trunks are open and gushing accessories and feathered folderols. These windows were a salute to Elton John and his costumes. Posters of Elton John appearances are methodically laid out on the floor while dozens of his photos line the walls. Everybody loves the color and shine of such theatricality!!

THEATER 159

BARNEYS, Madison Ave., New York, NY
Creative Director: Simon Doonan
Sr. VP of Creative Services: David New
VP of Creative Services: Adamo DiGregerio

ZCMI, Salt Lake City, UT
Display Director:
Mike Stephens
Designer: Alysa Revell

ZCMI saluted the opening of the Ballet Season with this "Swan Lake"-ish setting of harlequin patterns and crinkly, silvery fabrics. The bronzed forms are in white net tutus except for the "prima ballerina" who is dressed in a sequin studded black tutu. The spotlight, up front, makes the announcement—"Point / Counterpoint" and the appearance of Ballet West in town. The Gala means getting all dressed up—and ZCMI has lots to offer.

Henri Bendel also took on the ballet theme to play up some black and white tops. The costumes shown are "antiques" and thus quite interesting in themselves. Added to these are the floating fruits, flowers and silvery accessories.

Macy's saluted a film festival. The poster was featured on the right and balanced by the line of mannequins on the left. The rear wall was systematically patterned with cut-out replicas of film reels—a recognizable symbol for movies.

From old-time radio to today's TV—the "Applause" sign is a familiar symbol. It acknowledges a job well done or the entrance of the featured players. Bergdorf playfully reproduces that sign and outlines it with red light bulbs to play up the entrance onto the scene of these new gowns.

HENRI BENDEL, Fifth Ave., New York, NY

THEATER 161

MACY'S, Herald Square, New York, NY
VP of VM: Marc Minichiello
Window Visual Director: Sam Joseph
Sr. Exec. of Windows: Gil Croy

BERGDORF GOODMAN, Fifth Ave., New York, NY
VP of Visual Presentation: Linda Fargo
Window Visual Dir.: David Hoey

Time marches on! It waits for no man or woman. It is always with us—always there to tell us that we must act or be left behind.

Saks takes time on the road. In a surreal compilation of unrelated objects the display gets our attention and stops us in our tracks. What is the lady in the evening gown doing with TV sets, an upturned clock and safety lights all chained onto a kiddie pull wagon? The floor is littered with electric cables and wires. What does it mean? What time is it?

There is no question as to what time it is in Lord & Taylor's New Year's Eve window. These mannequins are dressed for the occasion and they've got a giant clock to watch for the count down. Note the clock—with a whole different time—cast by a gobo on the rear right wall.

SAKS FIFTH AVE., New York, NY
V.P. of V. M.: Ken Smart
Dir. of Windows: Randy Yaw

LORD & TAYLOR, Fifth Ave., New York, NY
Dir. of Windows, N.Y.: Jan Topercer
Creative Director: Manoel Renha

CHANEL, E. 57th St., New York, NY
Display: Todd Schearer

MARSHALL FIELD, State St., Chicago, IL
V.M. Dir., State St., Amy Meadows
Design: Tracy Hachler / Sue Hawks

Chanel proudly introduces La Ronde: its new designer watch. In a predominantly black, gray and white window, the gold face of the photo on the lower right gets the attention and brings the viewer's eye down to the name printed on the front glass.

Swatch makes a Valentine appeal with a papier mache delivery boy holding a watch in one hand and a greeting card in the other. The red flowers on the floor complete the message.

To introduce the Kenneth Cole new line of watches, the people at Marshall Field masked the window down to a shadow box more in proportion to the product on display. This also focuses the viewer on to what really matters. The "dynamite" theme plays well. The sticks of "dynamite" serve to show off the watches and the watch bands and with the nickel plated chains plays as an amusing foil for the watches and chains shown on the floor.

SWATCH, E. 57th St., New York, NY

PRADA, (RIGHT AND BELOW) Madison Ave. and Bellagio, Las Vegas, NV

Getting there can be half the fun—and planning how to get there can be the rest.

Prada is traveling in high style by car and luxury train. Working in open back windows, the designers have created shopper-stopping displays. Who needs all the wheels, the front of the car or any more of the train when the "suggestion" tells the whole story?

For the more adventurous there is always the motor bike, bi-ped or scooter. Bloomingdale's plays up the daring, red Kate Spade bag by taking it for an outing on a sleek, virile black motor bike. Bergdorf's Store for Men enhances the Italian styling of Gucci by showing the stylized male mannequin astride the Italian bi-ped as it "rides" over red/white/green striped fluorescent tubes stretched across the floor.

TRAVELING ON 165

BLOOMINGDALES, Lexington Ave., New York, NY
VP of Visual Merchandising: Jack Hruska
Creative Director: Mike Fisher
Window Manager: Harry Medina

BERGDORF GOODMAN, STORE FOR MEN,
Fifth Ave., New York, NY
VP of Visual Merchandising: Linda Fargo
Window Director: David Hoey

MACY'S, (TOP AND ABOVE) **Herald Square, New York, NY**
Window Visuals Director: Sam C. Joseph
Sr. Executive for Windows/VM: Gil Croy
Photographer: James Mulea

Located in the heart of Manhattan within the shadow of the Empire State Building, who would know more about Urban Living and the Urban Look than the people at Macy's? Shown here are some recent displays in which Macy's promoted urban fashions and particular urban fashion lines.

It is "Urban Evolution" with an explosion of color, graffiti and a rear wall papered with posters; it is the sort of sight you see anywhere a construction fence goes up and poster paster-uppers are set loose. To further enhance the street theme, a panel of cyclone fencing, up front, appears to place one of the mannequins in a play area. In keeping with the look and the poster art all the mannequins have stylized red wigs—the color of the "evolution." FUBU, a collection of street-wise fashions, was presented in several of Macy's windows. This hip and hot selection of garments for boys and young men is shown amid yellow painted garbage cans and discarded tires in an all-white setting. The checkerboard panel, on the rear wall, is multi-colored and the squares are filled with line drawings/cartoons of the FUBU market.

Marshall Field in Chicago came up with their own Urban Look for their "Kenneth Cole Reaction" display. The simple, symmetrical setting gets the "street" look from the gray grill back panel and the floor grid—as well as the "body language" of the semi-abstract mannequins. The glowing red light, center, adds a colored accent.

URBAN LOOK 167

MACY'S, Herald Square, New York, NY
Window Visuals Director: Sam C. Joseph
Sr. Executive for Windows/VM: Gil Croy
Photographer: James Mulea

LORD & TAYLOR, Fifth Ave., New York, NY
Creative Director: Manoel Renha
Designer: Jan Topercer

Webs make one think of spiders and spiders play their part in creating spooky, chilling atmospheres for Halloween windows. But, webs are also used to snare and trap and to attract, beguile, confine and eventually engulf the unsuspecting. Shown here are some web-works that vary from the spider's intricate pattern to the pattern devised by displaypersons to attract, beguile, entangle and eventually "sell" the product.

The delicate spider's web behind the form in the red/gold glowing Lord & Taylor window is another of that company's salutes to the Halloween holiday.

Barneys is intrigued with, and in love with, the fanciful weavings that enmesh an entire window and the mannequins trapped amidst the threads. In one display, feathers, flowers and foliage are caught up in the maze as well as the plaid clad abstracts while in the others the designers have used the involved patterns to create settings for the mannequins. Note how fish net has been used to create the "webbing" by the clever stretching, pulling and tying down the web-like fabric in the window space.

BARNEYS, Madison Ave., New York, NY
Creative Director: Simon Doonan
Sr. VP of Creative Services: David New
VP of Creative Services: Adamo DiGregerio

WEB-WORK 169

BARNEYS, (TOP AND ABOVE) Madison Ave., New York, NY
Creative Director: Simon Doonan
Sr. VP of Creative Services: David New
VP of Creative Services: Adamo DiGregerio

MOSCHINO, Madison Ave., New York, NY
Display Director: David Griffin

LORD & TAYLOR, Fifth Ave., New York, NY
Creative Director: Manoel Renha
Director of V.M., Fifth Ave.: Jan Topercer

Wire: bendable, pliable, twistable and curvable. What can't you do with wire? It doesn't have to be welded—though it can be. Illustrated here are a variety of wire work wonders.

Fabric ribbon-covered bands of wire become the hooped skirt frame that support the Moschino tops. Note the amusing placement of the shoes under the skirt and how they have been highlighted. Who needs a real skirt when the wire frame one does so much for the display.

Lord & Taylor combines metal rectangular frames with glistening wire mesh that seems to wrap the mannequins' heads in flying, floating and flashing metallic strands. In an otherwise static display, the convoluted wirework streamers create a moving experience.

Barneys' oversized wire hangers, simply twisted and tied, become the supporting elements for the dangling mannequin legs and arms in another surreal take on display.

The Bergdorf for Men's display features twisted wire circus performers—in miniature—on the floor and tightrope walking across the back of the window. A circus cage, on the floor, can accommodate some of the animals prowling amid the spools of thread. Note the spool-of-thread carousel on the floor, left.

BARNEYS, (TOP AND ABOVE) Madison Ave., New York, NY
Creative Director: Simon Doonan
Sr. V.P. Creative Services: David New
V.P. of Creative Services: Adamo Di Gregorio

BERGDORF FOR MEN, Fifth Ave., New York, NY
Window Director: Harry Bader

HERMES, E. 57th St., New York, NY
Display Director: Eric Werner

It appears that Hermes is really ready for a cold, cold winter. Not only do they have the coat and accessories to fight off the chilling breezes, they have stacked their window with enough cut and dried wood to keep the fireplace going and going and going. The sharp green niches add an almost spring-like quality to this "brrr" window. Note how the natural beige toned wood also plays up the color of the coat.

Max Mara highlights wood tones. The photo blow-up shows a mannequin in a black suit seated on a wood covered cube in a wood paneled setting. The actual suit is shown up front and off-center on a dress form and it is backed up by another blow-up that features a variety of woods and wood finishes.

Tiffany's, in Munich, used driftwood or any other old, dried out, natural wood growths to create a series of desert-like settings—complete with bleached animal skulls. These windows were designed to feature men's watches. The puddles of pale sand and the ivory colored skulls—all smooth and shiny—complement the rough texture of the wood.

WOOD 173

MAX MARA, Madison Ave., New York, NY

TIFFANY'S, (LEFT AND ABOVE) Munich, Germany
Design: Deko Rank, Peter Rank

BERGDORF FOR MEN,
(ABOVE AND RIGHT) **Fifth Ave.,
New York, NY
Visuals Director: Harry Bader**

Wood works or works of wood art/sculpture are used in the Bergdorf for Men displays shown here. The store has selected giant plywood cut-out and notched-together dragons and/or dinosaurs to dress up the featured men's wear shown casually draped/dressed on suit forms. These notched super sculptures look like children's dinosaur kits that are simply put together.

Index

A
Aston & Gunn, 22, 25
A. Testoni, 93

B
Bally's, 36, 104
Barneys, 14, 27, 40, 46, 59, 72, 81, 94, 95, 110, 112, 119, 125, 130, 134, 135, 142, 145, 151, 159, 168, 169, 171
Bergdorf Goodman, 13, 15, 17, 24, 26, 36, 45, 52, 53, 56, 70, 76, 80, 88, 89, 92, 103, 106, 111, 113, 117, 118, 137, 154, 155, 161, 165, 171, 174
Birks Jewelers, 32, 33, 47, 98, 99, 140, 141, 148, 149
Bloomingdales, 17, 35, 57, 71, 78, 83, 85, 136, 145, 150, 152, 156, 165
Book Store, The, 47
Burberrys, 25, 28, 29, 51, 57, 59

C
C&A, 133
Cada, 27, 40, 48, 82
Carson Pirie Scott, 42, 43, 123
Cecile, 21, 69
Chanel, 115, 163
Christian Dior, 68, 75
Cole Haan, 93, 130

D
Daffys, 18, 131
DKNY, 158
Dolce & Gabbana, 25
Dooney & Burke, 73

E
Ermenegildo Zegna, 46
Escada, 97

F
Ferregamo, 39, 65, 105, 125
Frohlich Furs, 139

G
Gap, The, 75
Gianfranco Ferre, 77
Gucci, 15, 37, 87, 112

H
Harrod's, 64
Henri Bendel, 10, 11, 31, 41, 86, 104, 129, 138, 144, 151, 160
Hermes, 34, 172
H&M, 133
Holland & Holland, 58
Hoya Crystal, 12

L
Lalique, 69
Liberty of London, 30
Lord & Taylor, 74, 79, 83, 114, 124, 126, 129, 146, 162, 168, 170
Loro Piano, 137, 143

M
Macy's, 20, 34, 37, 47, 62, 63, 75, 81, 89, 161, 166, 167
Marshall Field, 16, 26, 84, 91, 105, 107, 128, 146, 163
Max Mara, 21, 39, 173
Miss Jackson's, 61
Moschino, 70, 96, 109, 115, 138, 142, 152, 157, 170

N
Nymphenburg Porzellan, 45

P
Palais Royale, 42
Paul Stuart, 93
Pilar Rossi, 23, 132
Prada, 116, 153, 164
Printemps, 133

S
Saks Fifth Avenue, 23, 31, 38, 45, 50, 60, 67, 91, 92, 102, 118, 120, 121, 127, 143, 145, 150, 156, 157, 162
Salvatore Ferregamo, 76
Sevigne, 55
Shanghai Tang, 12
Sherle Wagner, 13, 19, 111
Sony Style, 147
St. John Boutique, 86, 87, 108
Swatch, 79, 163

T
T. Eaton & Co., 22, 77, 91, 100, 101, 122
Tiffany, 48, 49, 54, 68, 73, 97, 139, 173

U
Uhren Huber, 20

V
Valentino, 66, 116
Versace, 131

W
Wathne, 125

Z
ZCMI, 44, 66, 82, 126, 127, 160
Zegna, 90, 114

The Visual Reference Library
of Architecture and Design

American Graphic Design Awards
Cafe Design
Cafes & Bistros
Cafes & Coffee Shops
Contemporary Exhibit Design
Corporate Interiors
Educational Environments
Entertainment Destinations
Entertainment Dining
Gourmet & Specialty Shops
Healthcare Spaces
Hospitality & Restaurant Design
Hot Graphics USA
Indonesian Accents
Point of Purchase Design Annual
Specialty Food Store Design
Storefronts & Facades
Stores of the Year
Store Windows
Streetscapes
The Power of Visual Presentation
Urban Spaces
Winning Shopping Center Designs

Visit

www.visualreference.com